First World War
and Army of Occupation
War Diary
France, Belgium and Germany

35 DIVISION
Divisional Troops
Royal Army Medical Corps
105 Field Ambulance
28 January 1916 - 24 April 1919

WO95/2478/1

The Naval & Military Press Ltd
www.nmarchive.com
Published in association with The National Archives

Published by

The Naval & Military Press Ltd

Unit 10 Ridgewood Industrial Park,

Uckfield, East Sussex,

TN22 5QE England

Tel: +44 (0) 1825 749494

www.naval-military-press.com

www.nmarchive.com

This diary has been reprinted in facsimile from the original. Any imperfections are inevitably reproduced and the quality may fall short of modern type and cartographic standards.

© Crown Copyright
Images reproduced by permission of The National Archives, London, England, 2015.

Contents

Document type	Place/Title	Date From	Date To
Heading	WO95/2478 Jan'16-Apr'19 105 Field Ambulance		
Heading	35th Division Medical 105th Fld Ambulance 1916 Jan-1919 Apr		
Heading	No 105 Field Ambulance Vol I Jan Feb 1916		
Heading	105th. Field Ambulance Vol I		
War Diary	Tidworth Salisbury Pla.	28/01/1916	28/01/1916
War Diary	Southampton	28/01/1916	28/01/1916
War Diary	Le Havre	28/01/1916	30/01/1916
War Diary	Blendecques	31/01/1916	31/01/1916
War Diary	Fousenghem	31/01/1916	08/02/1916
War Diary	Wardrecques	08/02/1916	18/02/1916
War Diary	Boeseghem	18/02/1916	19/02/1916
War Diary	Calonne	19/02/1916	27/02/1916
Heading	35th Div 105 FA Vol 293. March 1914 April 1916 Div 18		
War Diary	Colonne	01/03/1916	13/03/1916
War Diary	Veille Chapelle	15/03/1916	25/03/1916
War Diary	Estaires	26/03/1916	25/04/1916
War Diary	Vieille Chapelle	27/04/1916	30/04/1916
Heading	35th Division No 105 Field Ambulance May 1916		
War Diary	Vieille Chapelle	01/05/1916	31/05/1916
Heading	140/1949. No.105. Field Ambulance. June 1916		
War Diary	Vieille Chapelle	01/06/1916	17/06/1916
War Diary	Bois Du Pacquot	18/06/1916	22/06/1916
War Diary	Bois Du Pacaut	22/06/1916	28/06/1916
War Diary	Orlencourt	29/06/1916	30/06/1916
Heading	35th Division War Diary of 105th. Field Ambulance from 1 July 1916 to 31 July 1916 Volume 6		
War Diary	Orlencourt	01/07/1916	03/07/1916
War Diary	Lucheux	04/07/1916	06/07/1916
War Diary	Bus Les Artois	07/07/1916	09/07/1916
War Diary	Lealvillers	10/07/1916	13/07/1916
War Diary	Morlancourt	14/07/1916	14/07/1916
War Diary	Happy Valley	15/07/1916	19/07/1916
War Diary	Talus Boise	20/07/1916	31/07/1916
Heading	War Diary 105th Field Ambulance RAMC. From 1st August 1916 to 31st August 1916 Volume VII		
War Diary	Happy Valley	01/08/1916	02/08/1916
War Diary	Sailly Le Sec	03/08/1916	05/08/1916
War Diary	Camp-En-Amienois	06/08/1916	10/08/1916
War Diary	Sailly Le Sec	10/08/1916	15/08/1916
War Diary	Happy Valley	16/08/1916	20/08/1916
War Diary	Billon Farm	20/08/1916	26/08/1916
War Diary	Citadel	27/08/1916	30/08/1916
War Diary	Candas	31/08/1916	31/08/1916
Heading	35th Div. 140/1817 War Diary 105th Field Ambulance R.A.M.C. 1st Sept 1916 to 30th Sept 1916. Inclusive. Volume VIII		
War Diary	Le Souich	01/09/1916	02/09/1916
War Diary	Lignereuil	03/09/1916	30/09/1916

Heading	War Diary of 105th Field Ambulance. R.A.M.C. From 1st October. 1916. to 31st October 1916 Inclusive. Volume IX. 35th Div		
War Diary	Lignereuil	01/10/1916	31/10/1916
Heading	War Diary. of 105th Field Ambulance. R.A.M.C. From 1st November 1916. To 30th November 1916. Inclusive. Volume X		
War Diary	Lignereuil	01/11/1916	30/11/1916
Heading	War Diary of 105th Field Ambulance From 1st December 1916. To 31st December 1916. Inclusive Volume XI 35th Div 140/1903		
War Diary	Lignereuil	01/12/1916	05/12/1916
War Diary	Maizieres	06/12/1916	31/12/1916
Heading	War Diary 105th Field Ambulance From 1st January 1917. To 31st January 1917. Inclusive. Volume. XII 35th Div. 140/1943		
War Diary	Maizieres.	01/01/1917	31/01/1917
Heading	War Diary of 105th Field Ambulance R.A.M.C. From 1st February 1917. To 28th February 1917 Inclusive. Volume. XIII 35th Div. 140/1997		
War Diary	Maizieres	01/02/1917	06/02/1917
War Diary	Ligny Sur Canche	07/02/1917	07/02/1917
War Diary	Occoches	08/02/1917	08/02/1917
War Diary	Vignacourt	09/02/1917	19/02/1917
War Diary	Marcelcave	20/02/1917	22/02/1917
War Diary	Le Quesnel Camp.	23/02/1917	28/02/1917
Heading	War Diary. of 105th Field Ambulance. R.A.M.C. From 1st March 1917. To 31st March 1917. Inclusive. Volume X V 35th Div.		
War Diary	Le Quesnel Camp.	01/03/1917	18/03/1917
War Diary	Rosieres	19/03/1917	29/03/1917
War Diary	Omiecourt	30/03/1917	31/03/1917
Heading	War Diary of 105th Field Ambulance R.A.M.C. From 1st April 1917 To 30th April 1917. Inclusive Volume. XV		
War Diary	Omiecourt	01/04/1917	01/04/1917
War Diary	Mesnil-St.-Nicaise.	02/04/1917	11/04/1917
War Diary	Tertry	11/04/1917	17/04/1917
War Diary	Vermand	18/04/1917	30/04/1917
Heading	War Diary of 105th Field Ambulance R.A.M.C. From 1st May 1917. To 31st May 1917. Inclusive. Volume XVI.		
War Diary	Vermand	01/05/1917	19/05/1917
War Diary	Peronne	20/05/1917	20/05/1917
War Diary	Fins	21/05/1917	31/05/1917
Miscellaneous	Appendix. XVth Corps Main Dressing Station. Summaries of Sick States.	20/05/1917	20/05/1917
Miscellaneous	XVth Corps Main Dressing Station. Summaries of sick states.	23/05/1917	23/05/1917
Miscellaneous	XVth Corps Main Dressing Station. Summaries of sick states.	26/05/1917	26/05/1917
Miscellaneous	XVth Corps Main Dressing Station. Summaries of sick states.	29/05/1917	29/05/1917
Heading	War Diary of 105th Field Ambulance. R.A.M.C. From. 1st June 1917. To 30th June 1917. Inclusive. Volume XVII		

War Diary	Fins.	01/06/1917	30/06/1917
Miscellaneous	Appendix. XVth Corps Main Dressing Station. Daily Sick States.	31/05/1917	31/05/1917
Miscellaneous	IIIrd Corps Main Dressing Station Daily Sick States.	03/06/1917	03/06/1917
Miscellaneous	III Corps Main Dressing Station. Daily Sick States.	06/06/1917	06/06/1917
Miscellaneous	III Corps Main Dressing Station. Daily Sick States.	09/06/1917	09/06/1917
Miscellaneous	III Corps Main Dressing Station. Daily Sick States.	12/06/1917	12/06/1917
Miscellaneous	IIIrd Corps Main Dressing Station. Daily Sick States.	15/06/1917	15/06/1917
Miscellaneous	IIIrd Corps Main Dressing Station. Daily Sick States.	18/06/1917	18/06/1917
Miscellaneous	IIIrd Corps Main Dressing Station. Daily Sick States.	21/06/1917	21/06/1917
Miscellaneous	IIIrd Corps Main Dressing Station. Daily Sick States.	24/06/1917	24/06/1917
Miscellaneous	IIIrd Corps Main Dressing Station. Daily Sick States.	27/06/1917	27/06/1917
Heading	War Diary of 105th Field Ambulance R.A.M.C. From 1st July 1917 To 31st July 1917. Inclusive Volume XVIII		
War Diary	III C.M.D.S Fins	01/07/1917	10/07/1917
War Diary	Longavesnes	10/07/1917	31/07/1917
Miscellaneous	III Corps Main Dressing Station. Daily Sick States.	30/06/1917	30/06/1917
Miscellaneous	III Corps Main Dressing Station. Daily Sick States.	03/07/1917	03/07/1917
Miscellaneous	IIIrd Corps Main Dressing Station. Daily Sick States.	06/07/1917	06/07/1917
Miscellaneous	IIIrd Corps Main Dressing Station. Daily Sick States.	09/07/1917	09/07/1917
Heading	War Diary. of 105th Field Ambulance R.A.M.C. From 1st August 1917. To 31st August 1917. Inclusive. Volume XIX		
War Diary	Longavesnes	01/08/1917	31/08/1917
Heading	War Diary of 105th Field Ambulance R.A.M.C. From 1st September 1917. to 30th September 1917 Inclusive Volume XX		
War Diary	Longavesnes	01/09/1917	29/09/1917
War Diary	Peronne	30/09/1917	30/09/1917
Heading	War Diary of 105 Field Ambulance R.A.M.C. From 1st October 1917. To 31st October 1917. Inclusive. Volume XXI		
War Diary	Peronne	01/10/1917	02/10/1917
War Diary	Lattre-St. Quentin Near Arras.	03/10/1917	03/10/1917
War Diary	Auesnes Le Comte	04/10/1917	08/10/1917
War Diary	Avesnes Le Comte Near Arras.	09/10/1917	13/10/1917
War Diary	Zeggars Capel. Sheet 27 B16C	14/10/1917	15/10/1917
War Diary	Crombeke	16/10/1917	18/10/1917
War Diary	Proven	19/10/1917	31/10/1917
Heading	War Diary. of 105th Field Ambulance. R.A.M.C. From 1st November 1917. To 30th November 1917. Inclusive. Volume XXII		
War Diary	W Camp A7d Central Sheet 28	01/11/1917	05/11/1917
War Diary	Purley Camp.	06/11/1917	07/11/1917
War Diary	Herzeele	08/11/1917	10/11/1917
War Diary	Herzeele D8C7.7	11/11/1917	15/11/1917
War Diary	Herzeele	16/11/1917	16/11/1917
War Diary	Essex Fm.	17/11/1917	30/11/1917
Heading	War Diary of 105th Field Ambulance. R.A.M.C. From. 1st December 1917. To 31st December 1917. Inclusive. Volume. XXIII		
War Diary	Essex Farm.	01/12/1917	08/12/1917
War Diary	Herzeele	09/12/1917	31/12/1917

Heading	War Diary. Of 105th. Field Ambulance. R.A.M.C. From 1st. January 1918. To 31st. January 1918. Inclusive. Volume XXIV. Original.		
War Diary	Herzeele Sheet 27 D9d9.7	01/01/1918	06/01/1918
War Diary	Canada Fm Sheet 28 A18a2.7	07/01/1918	07/01/1918
War Diary	Canada Farm.	08/01/1917	31/01/1917
Heading	War Diary Of 105th. Field Ambulance. R.A.M.C. From 1st. February 1918. To 28th. February 1918. Inclusive. Volume XXV. Original.		
War Diary	Canada Farm Sheet 28 A18a2.7	01/02/1918	13/02/1918
War Diary	Canada Farm	14/02/1918	28/02/1918
Heading	War Diary Of 105th. Field Ambulance R.A.M.C. From 1st. March 1918. To 31st. March 1918. Inclusive Volume XXVI. Original.		
War Diary	Canada Farm Sheet 28 A18A2.7	01/03/1918	08/03/1918
War Diary	Canada Farm.	09/03/1918	24/03/1918
War Diary	Cerisy 62D. Q8c	24/03/1918	25/03/1918
War Diary	Sailly-Le Sec. 62D J28d.	26/03/1918	26/03/1918
War Diary	Warloy Baillon Amiens 1/100,000. G6,3.1	27/03/1918	30/03/1918
War Diary	Lahoussoye 62D 18b9.9	31/03/1918	31/03/1918
Heading	War Diary Of 105th. Field Ambulance R.A.M.C. From 1st. April 1918. To 30th. April 1918. Inclusive Volume XXVII. Original.		
War Diary	Lahoussoye	01/04/1918	06/04/1918
War Diary	Toutencourt.	07/04/1918	07/04/1918
War Diary	Varennes	08/04/1918	23/04/1918
War Diary	Varennes.	25/04/1918	30/04/1918
Heading	War Diary Of 105th. Field Ambulance R.A.M.C. From 1st. May 1918 To 31st. May 1918 Inclusive Volume XXVIII. Original.		
War Diary	Varennes Sheet 57D P25d3.3	01/05/1918	02/05/1918
War Diary	Herissart T10a3.4.	03/05/1918	06/05/1918
War Diary	Herissart	07/05/1918	19/05/1918
War Diary	Toutencourt	20/05/1918	22/05/1918
War Diary	Talmas 57DS3d2.6	23/05/1918	29/05/1918
War Diary	Talmas.	30/05/1918	31/05/1918
Heading	War Diary Of 105th. Field Ambulance R.A.M.C. From 1st. June 1918. To 30th. June 1918. Inclusive. Volume XXIX. Original.		
War Diary	Talmas 57DS3d2.6	01/06/1918	30/06/1918
Heading	War Diary Of 105th. Field Ambulance R.A.M.C. From 1st. July 1918 To 31st. July 1918 Inclusive Volume XXX. Original.		
War Diary	Talmas 57D 1/40,000 S3d 2.6	01/07/1918	01/07/1918
War Diary	St Martin/Laert	02/07/1918	02/07/1918
War Diary	Watou 27 1/40,000 K4b8.5	03/07/1918	03/07/1918
War Diary	Watou	04/07/1918	04/07/1918
War Diary	Terdighem P10a9.1	05/07/1918	06/07/1918
War Diary	Terdighem	07/07/1918	08/07/1918
War Diary	Wagenbruge Fm P12J2.3	09/07/1918	15/07/1918
War Diary	Terdinghem	16/07/1918	31/07/1918
Heading	War Diary. Of 105th Field Ambulance. From 1st August 1918. To 31st August 1918. Inclusive. Volume XXXI. Original.		
War Diary	St Sylvestre Cappel. Sheet 27 (P22d9.2)	29/08/1918	30/08/1918
War Diary	1 Mile E. of Eecke	31/08/1918	31/08/1918

War Diary	St Sylvestre Cappel	31/08/1918	31/08/1918
War Diary	St Sylvestre Cappel Sheet 27 (P22d9.2.)	20/08/1918	28/08/1918
War Diary	St Sylvestre Cappel. Sheet 27 (P22d9.2)	11/08/1918	20/08/1918
War Diary	Wagenbruge Sheet 27 (P12.d2.3.)	09/08/1918	09/08/1918
War Diary	St Sylvestre Cappel Sheet 27 (P22d9.2.)	10/08/1918	11/08/1918
War Diary	Wagenbruge. Sheet 27 (P.12d2.3.)	01/08/1918	08/08/1918
Heading	War Diary. Of 105th Field Ambulance. R.A.M.C. From 1st September 1918. To 30th September 1918. Inclusive. Volume. XXXII. Original.		
War Diary	Moore Park Farm 28/G4d4.4	04/09/1918	11/09/1918
War Diary	St. Sylvestre Cappel Sheet 27. (P.22d9.2)	01/09/1918	02/09/1918
War Diary	Scout Camp	02/09/1918	03/09/1918
War Diary	Moore Park Farm. 28/G4d4.4	12/09/1918	16/09/1918
War Diary	Brandhoek. 28/G12b7.7.	17/09/1918	30/09/1918
Heading	War Diary. Of 105th Field Ambulance. R.A.M.C. From 1st October 1918. To 31st October 1918. Inclusive. Volume. XXXIII. Original.		
War Diary	Brandhoek Sheet 28 G12b7.7.	01/10/1918	17/10/1918
War Diary	Ecole. Ypres 28/I9C.	18/10/1918	20/10/1918
War Diary	Bisseghem. 29/G35a8.2	20/10/1918	30/10/1918
War Diary	Sweveghem. 29 (O.1d2.6)	30/10/1918	31/10/1918
Heading	War Diary Of 105th. Field Ambulance R.A.M.C. 1st. November 1918 To 30th. November 1918. Inclusive. Volume XXXIV. Original.		
War Diary	Sweveghem Sheet O.1.d.2.6	01/11/1918	07/11/1918
War Diary	Staceghem 29/H.30.c5.9	07/11/1918	10/11/1918
War Diary	Ingoyghem 29/p.3b1.7.	11/11/1918	13/11/1918
War Diary	Berchem 29 (Q21C2.7)	14/11/1918	19/11/1918
War Diary	Heule.	19/11/1918	28/11/1918
War Diary	Menin.	29/11/1918	29/11/1918
War Diary	Vlamertinghe	30/11/1918	30/11/1918
Heading	War Diary. of 105th Field Ambulance. R.A.M.C. From 1st December 1918. To 31st December 1918. Inclusive Volume. XXXV. Original.		
War Diary	Steenvoorde	01/12/1918	01/12/1918
War Diary	Pelderhouck	02/12/1918	02/12/1918
War Diary	Watten (L.14.a9.9)	03/12/1918	31/12/1918
Heading	War Diary Of 105th. Field Ambulance. R.A.M.C. From 1st. January 1919. To 31st. January 1919. Inclusive. Volume. XXXVI Original.		
War Diary	Watten.	01/01/1919	31/01/1919
Heading	War Diary of 105th. Field Ambulance. RAMC From 1st. February 1919. To 28th. February 1919. Inclusive. Volume XXXVII. Original		
War Diary	Watten.	01/02/1919	28/02/1919
Heading	War Diary Of 105th. Field Ambulance From 1st. March 1919. To 31st. March 1919. Inclusive. Volume. XXXVIII. Original.		
War Diary	Watten.	01/03/1919	31/03/1919
Heading	War Diary Of 105th. Field Ambulance. From April 1st. 1919. To April 24th. 1919. Inclusive. Volume XXXIV. Original		
War Diary	Watten.	01/04/1919	18/04/1919
War Diary	Dunkirk	19/04/1919	24/04/1919

WO 95/2478 (1)
Jan '16 - Apr '19
105 Field Ambulance

35TH DIVISION
MEDICAL

105TH FLD AMBULANCE
~~FEB 1916 - DEC 1918~~
1916 JAN — 1919 APL

No 105 Field Ambulance

Vol I

105th Field Ambulance

Vol I

Army Form C. 2118

WAR DIARY
or
INTELLIGENCE SUMMARY

(Erase heading not required.) 105 FIELD AMBULANCE

Instructions regarding War Diaries and Intelligence Summaries are contained in F.S. Regs., Part II. and the Staff Manual respectively. Title Pages will be prepared in manuscript.

Place	Date	Hour	Summary of Events and Information	Remarks and references to Appendices
Tidworth Salisbury Plain	28/1/16	2.30 p.m.	Departed from Leopardstown Station.	
Southampton	28/1/16	4 p.m.	Field Ambulance arrived.	
"	28/1/16	5 p.m.	1st Party (135 men 4 officers) left on the "Caesarea"	
"	"	7.45 p.m.	2nd Party (remainder of personnel, all horses & vehicles) left on "Lily of Dunkerk".	
Le Havre	"	11.30 p.m.	1st part arrived	
"	29/1/16	9 p.m.	2nd part arrived	
"	"	12 p.m.	Proceed to rest camp.	
"	30/1/16	1 p.m.	Left rest camp to entrain at Pont 2 gare des marchandise	
"	"	6 p.m.	Departed from Le Havre	
St Pierre	31/1/16	2.20 a.m.	Arrived & detrained.	
Fauquembergues	"	2.30 a.m.	Arrived & went into billets	
Lamhem	8/2/16	3.30 a.m.	Departed	
Nordausques	8/2/16	2 a.m.	Arrived	
"	11/2/16	10 a.m.	Inspection by F.M. Lord Kitchener	
"	18/2/16	10.30 a.m.	Departed	
Boeseghem	18/2/16	4 p.m.	Arrived & went into billets.	
	19/2/16	9.30 a.m.	Took over field work	
Robecq	19/2/16	2 p.m.	Arrived	

WAR DIARY
or
INTELLIGENCE SUMMARY

(Erase heading not required.)

Army Form C. 2118

Place	Date	Hour	Summary of Events and Information	Remarks and references to Appendices
Calonne	20/4/16	10.30am	C section of F.A. proceeded to ESTAIRES. Attached to 58th F.A. for instructional purposes night patrol scouted lights of posts. Parades of neighbourhood cart explored, flat low lying ground waterlogged, Camp with running water. Hospital land to the situated in Cheery mill.	
Lorme	21/4/16	10.30 am	C section of F.A. returned from Estaires. A section F.A. proceeded to Little Chapelle to be attached to 131st F.A. for instructional purposes. Included in party was the following officers Capt. J.G Thomas. Lieut W.W ally and Lieut ? horton.	

J.P Richard. Major R.A.M.C
O.C 105 = Field Ambulance ?

35th Div

10 S F U
Vol 23.

March 1916
April 1916

COMMITTEE FOR THE
MEDICAL HISTORY OF THE WAR
Date 9-JUN.1915

WAR DIARY or INTELLIGENCE SUMMARY

Army Form C. 2118

(Erase heading not required.)

105th Field Ambulance

Place	Date	Hour	Summary of Events and Information	Remarks and references to Appendices
Calonne	1/3/16		Nothing to report.	
"	2/3/16	2.30 p.m.	Major Rickard R.A.M.C. returned from Course of instruction with 130th Field Amb. at Hesdigneul.	
"	3/3/16		Nothing to report.	
"	4/3/16		Nothing to report.	
"	5/3/16	10.30 a.m.	B section F.A. proceeded to Estaires to be attached to 58th Field Ambulance for Course of instruction. Two officers Lieuts. D.J. McAfee and MacRury and forty men detailed for this duty.	
"	6/3/16		Corporal Geraghty and three men detached from the party at Lestrem to take over baths at X.11.t.4.3.	
"	7/3/16	11 a.m.	Proceeded to VIEILLE CHAPELLE, ST VAAST advanced dressing station and advanced post in connection Vy factory aid post & Plum Street aid post to inspect preparatory to taking over.	
"	8/3/16		Nothing to report.	
"	9/3/16		" "	
"	10/3/16	10 a.m.	Capt. Hegarty, one N.C.O. and 14 men with 3 G.S. wagons proceeded to VIEILLE CHAPELLE as an advance party.	
"	11/3/16	2.15 p.m.	Four men proceeded to S8a89 to take over baths.	
"	13/3/16	8.30 a.m.	Left Calonne, baths and hospital handed over to 107th Fd. Amb. Proceeded to VIEILLE CHAPELLE arriving 11 a.m.	
Vieille Chapelle	15/3/16	4 p.m.	Lieuts. McAfee and MacRury returned to Vieille Chapelle from Advanced dressing station at ST VAAST. Capt Hegarty and party proceeded to St Vaast A.D.S.	

WAR DIARY or INTELLIGENCE SUMMARY

Army Form C. 2118

105th FIELD AMBULANCE

Place	Date	Hour	Summary of Events and Information	Remarks and references to Appendices
NEUVE CHAPELLE	18/3/16	10 A.M.	Lieut Mackay and 30 men proceed to ANNEZIN as an advanced party.	
"	22.3.16		Lieut Mackay and 30 men recalled from Annezin. Lieut Morton and Lieut Donovan and 31 men replaced Capt Hegarty and Lieut Frost and 31 men at St VAAST advanced dressing station.	
"	24.3.16		St VAAST advanced dressing station and talks at RICHEBOURG handed over to 58th Fd Amb.	
"	25.3.16		Main dressing station at NEUVE CHAPELLE handed over to 131st Fd Amb. Fd. Amb. proceeded to Collège du Sacré Cœur at ESTAIRES. Lieut. Donovan and 12 men proceeded to A.D.S. at LAVENTIE.	
ESTAIRES	26.3.16		Lieut. Mackay and 26 men took over Divisional Bath & Laundry at ESTAIRES. Lieut Morton & 18 men proceeded to A.D.S. Laventie, taken over from 24 Fd Amb. Ecole St Louis and stores taken over & guard of 1 NCO & 5 men placed in charge. Officers Hospital (the Château) also taken over.	
"	27.3.16			
"	28.3.16 29.3.16 30.3.16 31.3.16		Simplest account for Laundry authority required to them in name of Lieut Mackay. NIL	G.W. Richard, Major R.A.M.C O.C. 105th Field Ambulance.

Army Form C. 2118

WAR DIARY
or
INTELLIGENCE SUMMARY
(Erase heading not required)

105th Field Ambulance Vol 3

G.W. Richard. Lt Col RAMC
O.C. 105th Fd Amb.

Place	Date	Hour	Summary of Events and Information	Remarks and references to Appendices
ESTAIRES	1.4.16		Lieut. McAfee proceeded to England on leave (11 days).	
"	2.4.16		NIL.	
"	3.4.16		NIL.	
"	4.4.16	10 a.m.	Capt. Fleming, Lieut. McAfoy and thirty one men proceeded to A.D.S. at Laventie relieving Lieuts. Donovan and Hunter and twenty five men who returned to Estaires	
"	5.4.16		NIL.	
"	6.4.16		NIL.	
"	7.4.16		NIL.	
"	8.4.16	9 a.m.	Capt. Hegarty and Lieut. Donovan proceeded to AIRE to attend lectures and demonstrations by the Chemical adviser to 1st Army. (8th and 9th inst.)	
"	9.4.16		NIL.	
"	10.4.16		NIL.	
"	11.4.16		NIL.	
"	12.4.16	10:30 a.m.	Capt. Hegarty and Lieut. Foyst proceeded to A.D.S. Laventie relieving Capt. Fleming and Lieut. McAfoy who returned to Estaires.	
"	13.4.16		NIL.	
"	14.4.16		NIL.	
"	15.4.16		Lieut. McAfee and Bowman proceeded to A.D.S. ST VAAST as advance party.	

G.W. Richard. Lt Col RAMC
O.C. 105th Fd Amb.

WAR DIARY
or
INTELLIGENCE SUMMARY

Army Form C. 2118

105th FIELD AMBULANCE

J.W. Richard. Lt Col R amc
O.C. 105th Fd Amb.

Place	Date	Hour	Summary of Events and Information	Remarks and references to Appendices
ESTAIRES	16.4.16		Lieut. Utley and 20 men proceeded to VIEILLE CHAPELLE as advance party. Divisional Bath and Laundry handed over to detachment of 107 Fd Amb. O.D.S. Lacontie handed over to detachment of 130 Fd Amb.	
"	17.4.16		Capt. Hegarty and Lieut. Firth and thirty seven men returned to Estaires. Unit proper moved as MO to 170 West-Yorks in place of Capt. Wilson Rames proceeded on leave. 105th Fd Amb moved from Estaires to Vieille Chapelle, taking over from 131st Fd Amb. Lieut. McAfee returned from St Vaast to Vieille Chapelle. One Cpl and 4 men took over Baths at Croix Bartee. Four men took over Baths at Richebourg St Vaast.	
"	18.4.16		nil.	
"	19.4.16		nil.	
"	20.4.16		nil.	
"	21.4.16		nil.	
"	22.4.16		Lt McAfee, Lt Thackeray and 30 men relieved Capt. Hegarty, Lt Firth and 30 men at advanced dressing station St VAAST.	
"	23.4.16		nil.	
"	24.4.16		nil.	
"	25.4.16		Lt Hunter returned unit from 17th West Yorks.	

Army Form C. 2118

WAR DIARY
or
INTELLIGENCE SUMMARY
(Erase heading not required.)

105 FIELD AMBULANCE

Instructions regarding War Diaries and Intelligence Summaries are contained in F. S. Regs., Part II. and the Staff Manual respectively. Title Pages will be prepared in manuscript.

Place	Date	Hour	Summary of Events and Information	Remarks and references to Appendices
VIEILLE CHAPELLE	27.4.16		Enemy shelled Vieille Chapelle during the afternoon; one English soldier, one French soldier and three civilians wounded; all but one civilian subsequently died.	
"	28.4.16		nil.	
"	29.4.16		Lt Doonan, Lt Hunter and 30 men relieved Lt. H. Eyles, Lt. Mackay & 20 men at A.D.S. ST VAAST.	
"	30.4.16		Lt. Mackay detailed O/C Baths.	

J.M. Richard Lt Col RAMC
O.C. 105 Field Ambulance

35th Division

No 105. Field Ambulance

May 1916.

105 FARE
Army Form C. 2118
Vol 4

WAR DIARY
or
INTELLIGENCE SUMMARY
(Erase heading not required.)

105th FIELD AMBULANCE.

Place	Date	Hour	Summary of Events and Information	Remarks and references to Appendices
VIEILLE CHAPELLE	1-5-16		Nil.	
	2-5-16		Nil.	
	3-5-16		Nil.	
	4-5-16		Inspection of horses by D.D.V.S.	
	5-5-16		Nil.	
	6-5-16		Capt. Fleming & Lieut. Mottley & 20 men relieved Lieut. Horton & Donovan & 20 men at A.D.S.	
	7-5-16		Lieut. Frost assumed duties of M.O. i/c 1/5th Northumberland Fusiliers vice Lt. Semipowers on leave.	
	8-5-16		Capt. Megaw proceeded on 7 days leave. Sanitary Exhibition opened at 105 F.A.	
	9-5-16		Staff Officers, C.O.s and others visited Exhibition. D.M.S. 1st Army visited A.D.S.	
	10-5-16		One steel cupola erected at St Vaast, two more commenced.	
	11-5-16		10 men proceeded to Green Barn A.D.S. to assist no working party. Hospl Hut proceeded to A.D.S.	
	12-5-16		15 men proceeded to A.D.S. to commence work of running dug outs.	
	13-5-16		Lieuts. McGee & MacRury relieved Capt. Fleming & Lieut. Mottley at A.D.S.	
	14-5-16		Nil	
	15-5-16		Inspection of unit by A.D.M.S. 35th Division	

Army Form C. 2118

WAR DIARY
or
INTELLIGENCE SUMMARY
(Erase heading not required.)

Instructions regarding War Diaries and Intelligence Summaries are contained in F.S. Regs., Part I and the Staff Manual respectively. Title Pa[ges] will be prepared in manuscript.

Place	Date	Hour	Summary of Events and Information	Remarks and references to Appendices
NEUVE CHAPELLE			105th FIELD AMBULANCE	
	16.5.16		12 men proceeded to A.D.S.	
	17.5.16		Sent Capt.L. sick to Factory Aid post. Capt. Hegarty returned from leave.	
	18.5.16		Lieut. Frost returned from duty with 15th Northumberland Fusiliers.	
	19.5.16		Two Cycles Completed at St Vaast and made gas proof.	
	20.5.16		Capt. Hegarty and Lieut. Frost proceeded to A.D.S. relieving Lieut. McAfee & Macrury.	
	21.5.16		NIL	
	22.5.16		NIL	
	23.5.16		Capt. Fleming proceed to LESTREM to act as D.A.D.M.S. during the absence on leave of Major Davidson.	
	24.5.16		NIL	
	25.5.16		NIL	
	26.5.16		NIL	
	27.5.16		Lieuts. Willey and Morton proceeded to A.D.S. relieving Capt. Hegarty & Lieut. Frost.	
	28.5.16		NIL	
	29.5.16		Lieut. Donovan returned from duty with 15th Cheshire Regiment.	
	30.5.16		Fifty wounded received from A.D.S. during the night. The majority evacuated to C.C.S.	
	31.5.16		NIL	

J M Richard Lt Col RAMC
O.C. 105th Field Ambulance

140/949.

No. 105. Field Ambulance.

COMMITTEE FOR THE
MEDICAL HISTORY OF THE WAR
Date 16 JUL. 1917

June 1916

WAR DIARY
INTELLIGENCE SUMMARY

105th FIELD AMBULANCE

Army Form C. 2118

Place	Date	Hour	Summary of Events and Information	Remarks and references to Appendices
VIEILLE CHAPELLE	1/6/16		Nothing to report	
	2/6/16		" " "	
	3/6/16		4 Officers and 62 other ranks of 2/2 South Midland Field Ambulance attached for instruction	
	4/6/16		61 Ordinaries attached for instruction. Lt McAFEE & Lt McRURY and 19 men proceeded to ST VAAST dressing station to relieve. Capt FLEMING returned from A.D.M.S's office. Capt WILKINSON and 20 other ranks of 2/2 FIELD AMBULANCE attached to advanced dressing station for instruction. Lt Col Q.H. RICHARD proceeded on leave. Capt T. FHEGARTY assumes temporary command. Nothing to report	
	5/6/16		" " "	
	6/6/16		" " "	
	7/6/16		" " "	
	8/6/16		Two more steel dug outs are being erected at ST VAAST	
	9/6/16		Nothing to report	
	10/6/16		Lt DONOVAN & L't MORTON relieved Lt McATEE & Lt McRURY at ST VAAST. L't W.W. UTTLEY proceeded on leave 2/2 Fd Amb. left after instruction	
	11/6/16		Nothing to report	
	12/6/16		" " "	
	13/6/16		" " "	

Army Form C. 2118

WAR DIARY
or
INTELLIGENCE SUMMARY
(Erase heading not required.)

105th FIELD AMBULANCE

Instructions regarding War Diaries and Intelligence Summaries are contained in F. S. Regs., Part II. and the Staff Manual respectively. Title Pages will be prepared in manuscript.

Place	Date	Hour	Summary of Events and Information	Remarks and references to Appendices
VIEILLE CHAPELLE	14/6/16		A steel dug out to be erected at the Baths at CROIX BARBEE	
	15/6/16		June advanced 60 minutes 11 pm becoming 12 pm	
	16/6/16		Nothing to report. Lt Col A H RICHARD returned from leave	
	17/6/16	2.30 pm	Advanced Dressing station ST VAAST handed over to 132nd Field Ambulance. Field Ambulance left VIEILLE CHAPELLE and proceeded to BOIS DU PACQUOT	
BOIS DU PACQUOT	18/6/16		arriving at 4.30 p.m. Nothing to report.	
"	19/6/16		Instructions received from A.D.M.S. to discard all surplus kit and equipment and to be ready to move at short notice. Lieut C.W. hacking Royal C placed under arrest and charged with when on Actors service, Drunkenness. Summary of Evidence and charge sheet prepared and forwarded to A.D.C. 105 th Infantry Brigade for necessary action. Lieut MTby returned from leave.	
"	20/6/16		Lieut McAfee proceeded to take over medical charge of 13th Cheshire in Lieut. Stewart proceed on 14 days leave of absence.	
"	21/6/16			
"	22.6.16		Capt Hegarty, Lieut Trout and one section of Field Ambulance proceeded to	

Army Form C. 2118

WAR DIARY
or
INTELLIGENCE SUMMARY

(Erase heading not required.)

105th FIELD AMBULANCE

Instructions regarding War Diaries and Intelligence Summaries are contained in F. S. Regs., Part II. and the Staff Manual respectively. Title Pages will be prepared in manuscript.

Place	Date	Hour	Summary of Events and Information	Remarks and references to Appendices
BOIS DU PACAUT	22.6.16	2.6.16	(Continued) Calonne and took over and established the school and mill as a hospital and itch depot. Also the baths. The Corporal and six men proceeded to ROBECQ to which the Field Ambulance sit there.	
	23.6.16	23.6.16	Nothing to report.	
	24.6.16		Court martial assembled for the purpose of trying No 43765 Pte Watson F. Ram C, charged with when on active service Drunkenness.	
	25.6.16		Proceedings of Court martial on Pte Watson returned, finding Guilty, Sentence 12 months imprisonment with Hard Labour. Promulgated at 6 p.m.	
	26.6.16		Ptes Turner, Jones and Skinner charged with "absent from billets from 9 p.m. to 11.35 p.m. on 25.6.16" awarded 7 days field punishment No 2.	
	27.6.16		Nothing to report.	
	28.6.16	7.15 p.m.	Handed over Calonne to 132nd Fd Ambt. Vacatn ROBECQ. Handed over patient at Bois du PACAUT to 133rd & 134th Fd Ambs. Left BOIS DU PACAUT. Marched at night via GONNEHEM, CHOCQUE, MARLES, DIVION and arrived at ORLENCOURT at 7 a.m. next day.	
ORLENCOURT	29.6.16		Nothing to report.	

WAR DIARY
or
INTELLIGENCE SUMMARY

(Erase heading not required.)

Army Form C. 2118

105th FIELD AMBULANCE

Place	Date	Hour	Summary of Events and Information	Remarks and references to Appendices
ORLENCOURT	30.5.16		Nothing to report.	

J.M. Richard
Lieut Col. RAMC
O.C. 105th Field Ambulance.

35th Division

Confidential

WAR DIARY
of
105th FIELD AMBULANCE

From 1 July 1916
to 31 July 1916

VOLUME 6

WAR DIARY
or
INTELLIGENCE SUMMARY

(Erase heading not required.)

105th FIELD AMBULANCE

Army Form C. 2118

Place	Date	Hour	Summary of Events and Information	Remarks and references to Appendices
ORLENCOURT	1.7.16		Nothing to report.	JMR
"	2.7.16		Orders received to be in readiness to move off at short notice.	JMR
"	3.7.16	4.30 a.m.	Unit moved from Orlencourt to LUCHEUX arriving at 4 p.m. 11.45 a.m.	JMR
LUCHEUX	4.7.16		Nothing to report	JMR
"	5.7.16		Lieut Holdfest returned from duty with the 16th Cheshires.	JMR
"	6.7.16	8.30 p.m.	Unit moved to BUS LES ARTOIS arriving at 3.15 a.m.	JMR
BUS LES ARTOIS	7.7.16		Took over Ambulance site from the 94th Field Ambulance. Sheds occupied by the men were flooded out by rain which fell continuously for 24 hours.	JMR
"	8.7.16		Nothing to report.	JMR
"	9.7.16	9 A.M.	Unit moved to LEALVILLERS arrived at 11.45 a.m. Court martial on Lieut MacRury R.A.M.C. assembled at 16.2 a.m. Witnesses for the prosecution Capt Fleming, Sergt Major Horton R.S.C. and Capt. Whitler R.A.M.C. Witnesses for the defence Capt Hegarty Lieuts MKee and Horton R.A.M.C. Capt. Hempshill R.A.M.C. O.C. 107th Fd Amb. acted as prosecutor.	JMR
LEALVILLERS	10.7.16		Nothing to report.	JMR
"	11.7.16		Proceeded to Montsaut, BOUZINCOURT and ALBERT with Capt. Fleming to inspect advanced dressing stations in view of the possibility of patients over the line.	JMR

WAR DIARY
or
INTELLIGENCE SUMMARY
(Erase heading not required.)

105 - FIELD AMBULANCE

Army Form C. 2118

Instructions regarding War Diaries and Intelligence Summaries are contained in F.S. Regs., Part II. and the Staff Manual respectively. Title Pages will be prepared in manuscript.

Place	Date	Hour	Summary of Events and Information	Remarks and references to Appendices
LEALVILLERS	12.7.16		Nothing to report.	AMR
"	13.7.16	2 pm	Moved to MORLANCOURT. Capt. Negus, Lieut. Coffey & 42 O.R. attached to 104th Brigade. One proceeded to Happy Valley Vat 10.15 a.m. Lieuts Hutton & Donovan & 10 O.R. proceeded to Corps Depot for stretcher-bearers, wounded at the Bray-Corbie road.	AMR
MORLANCOURT	14.7.16		C.O. Capt-Thomas & 36 men joined the Bearer Subdivision with 104th Brigade. Tent Subdivision under command 2 Lieut. Nutley proceeded to Corbie Chateau. Motor Ambulances reported for duty to O.C. Gwan Hussars Station at Sappers Corner. XIII Corps Rest Station at Corbie Chateau taken over in conjunction with 106 F.A.	AMR
HAPPY VALLEY	15.7.16		Lieut. Ford joined Bearer Subdivision. And the same evening was evacuated sick to Corbie C.C.S. Capt Hegarty detailed as M.O. to Heavy Siege Battery as a temporary measure. Nothing to report.	AMR
"	16.7.16		Bearer Subdivision proceeded to Billon wood.	AMR
"	17.7.16		Bearer Subdivision proceeded to MARICOURT. Sent to Coys 8 50 men & named for 36 hours & proceeded to BERNAFAY & TRONES wood to assist in clearing the front-line of wounded; the remainder of Bearers proceeded to TALUS BOISE with 104th Bg.di. Tent Subdivision proceeded to the Gwan Hussars Station at DIVES COPSE. Capt. J.B. Sen. of 106 F.A. temporarily attached to Tent Subdivision for duty.	AMR
"	19.7.16			AMR

WAR DIARY or INTELLIGENCE SUMMARY

Army Form C. 2118

(Erase heading not required.)

105 FIELD AMBULANCE

Place	Date	Hour	Summary of Events and Information	Remarks and references to Appendices
TALUS, BOISE	20.7.16		Lieut D. Kennedy posted to 105 Fd Amb. for duty and joined at Dives Copse. 10 O.R. proceeded to Corps Depot for bearers, wounded marched to BRONFAY farm.	MR
	21.7.16		7th Corps 9.50 men reported bearer subdivision at Talus Boise. 1 Lt Kennedy joined bearer subdivision from Dives Copse. Collecting post established at the BRIQUETERIE in conjunction with 106 & 107 Fd Amb. Two officers & 40 men proceeded to collecting post for 24 hours spell at intervals of 48 hours at first. Later 36 hours. Cases cleared to MARICOURT & CARNOY Advanced Dressing Stations.	MR
	22.7.16 23.7.16 24.7.16		A Corpl num ber of wounded brought to A.D.S. Pte Etherington & more killed at Talus Boise by shell fire at 4 p.m. Pte Forsyth killed by shell fire at 3 a.m. Lt/Sgt. after rejoining the bearers after going to Dublin collecting post in response to call for stretcher-bearers. Cpl. Hennon proceeded further to Bernafay wood and Dr. Davis Sgt. The Regimental M.O. were sent so he could be suitably brought to ground he organized the evacuation of wounded and carried on in their place. Pte Brine wounded at Talus Boise & evacuated.	MR MR MR
	25.7.16		Lieut Withey evacuated sick with French Firm to No 5 C.C.S. at Corbie. Capt Ralph "splits Turk" open Chas(?) of tent Supervising.	MR
	26.7.16 27.7.16 28.7.16		Bravery duly noted. Engaged in clearing cases from Dublin to Talus Boise. Pte Todd proceeded to by man third to recover the body of Capt. Hamilton 18.F. in response to a request from	MR

WAR DIARY
or
INTELLIGENCE SUMMARY

(Erase heading not required.)

Army Form C. 2118

105th FIELD AMBULANCE

Place	Date	Hour	Summary of Events and Information	Remarks and references to Appendices
TALUS BOISE	28/7/16		The O.C. 104th Brigade, he succeeded in reaching the body & organs it out of the shell hole in which it was buried. He carried it 40 yards under shell & sniper's fire but owing to the increasing of the fire was unable to carry it further. He gained the trenches with the object of getting a stretcher & someone to assist him, however no stretchers were available & the Company refused to allow any of his men to risk their lives. Lt. Thurlow abandoned it, the body was recovered later at night & brought down by bearers & TALUS BOISE and buried in Carnoy Cemetery.	JMR
"	29/7/16		Moved up to Convt. hauled by Lieut. McEvoy received and promulgated Further Inst. Sentence to be dismissed His Majesty's Service. He proceeded to the Base at 6 p.m. Horse transport moved back to Billon Wood owing to constant shelling.	JMR
	30/7/16		Ptes. Cowper, Willis & McCann were wounded at Dublin Collecting Post & evacuated. Ptes. Mulligan, Collinge & Page were wounded & bruised by a shell, he wounds well slight & they remained at duty. Pte. Priest evacuated suffering from shell shock. A large num. of cases were dealt with at the collecting post during the night & the following day. During the early hours of the morning the relay posts manned by the bearers were severely shelled, it was then that the bearers mentioned above were	JMR

WAR DIARY
or
INTELLIGENCE SUMMARY

(Erase heading not required.)

Army Form C. 2118

105th FIELD AMBULANCE

Place	Date	Hour	Summary of Events and Information	Remarks and references to Appendices
TALUS, BOISE	30/7/16		buried some of the other graves were shaken & demolished & shewd an inclination to divert their roots. Capt Flanyong therefore went up from the collecting post in Dublin Trench in spite of the shell fire which was being carried on over all the area, visited all the relay posts and by his coolness & inspiring example succeeded in rallying the men. Amongst the batteries at and near TALUS BOISE a considerable number of casualties occurred from time to time due to hostile shelling which often became intense, nearly all these cases were seen by Capt Fleming who never hesitated to expose himself in the open or take any risk or trek in order to tend these wounded men. I'm indeed other occasions this officer shewed remarkable devotion to duty under the most trying conditions.	MR
"	30/7/16		At 2 p.m. word was brought by a Chaplain that several wounded men were lying out unattended in the front line, these men apparently could not be dealt with by the stretcher bearers on the spot because they belonged to another Division, there upon Corp Bull & Pte Amesan went up and attempted to get wounded, three of whom they rescued from no mans land where they had been for two days. At 6 p.m. handed over to reserve subdivision of 55th Fd Amb & proceeded to Happy Valley with 104th Brigade.	MR

GM Richard Lt Col Comd
D.C. 105 Field Ambulance

Confidential

War Diary

105th Field Ambulance, R.A.M.C.

From 1st August 1916.
to
31st August 1916

35th Div.

Volume VII

August 1916

Army Form C. 2118

WAR DIARY
or
INTELLIGENCE SUMMARY
(Erase heading not required.)

105th FIELD AMBULANCE

Place	Date	Hour	Summary of Events and Information	Remarks and references to Appendices
HAPPY VALLEY	1.8.16		Nothing to report	JMR
	2.8.16	7 p.m.	Bearer Subdivision moved from Happy Valley to Sailly Le Sec	JMR
SAILLY LE SEC	3.8.16		Lieuts. Turton & Dowman with 20 men rejoined unit from Bonfay Farm. Tent Subdivision moved from Dives Copse to SAILLY LE SEC. Motor Ambulances rejoined unit.	JMR
"	4.8.16	1 p.m.	Horse transport under Capt. Hegarty marched with transport of 104th Brigade to VECQUEMONT.	JMR
"	5.8.16	4 A.M.	Horse transport moved to CAMP-EN-AMIENOIS. Field Ambulance marched to MERICOURT. Entrained at 10 A.M. Detrained at SALEUX at 1.30 p.m. and marched to CAMP-EN-AMIENOIS arriving at 6.15 p.m. Re-fittings of unit proceeded with.	JMR JMR
CAMP-EN-AMIENOIS	6.8.16			JMR JMR
"	7.8.16		Nothing to report.	JMR
"	8.8.16		Nothing to report.	JMR
"	9.9.16	6 A.M.	Capt Hegarty & all horse transport left to proceed with 107th Bde Brigade transport to VECQUEMONT	JMR YFH
"	10.8.16	5.30 AM	Personnel Field Ambulance marched to AIRIANES entrained at 8.30 AM detrained at CORBIE and marched to SAILLY LE SEC arriving at 1.30 P.M.	YFH

WAR DIARY
or
INTELLIGENCE SUMMARY

(Erase heading not required.)

Army Form C. 2118

Instructions regarding War Diaries and Intelligence Summaries are contained in F.S. Regs., Part II. and the Staff Manual respectively. Title Pages will be prepared in manuscript.

Place	Date	Hour	Summary of Events and Information	Remarks and references to Appendices
CAMPS EN AMIENOIS	10.5.16	8.30 AM	Motor transport arrived & went to SAILLY LE SEC arriving at 3 PM Horse transport proceeded to SAILLY LE SEC arriving at 11.30 AM	77 H
SAILLY LE SEC	"	3.30 PM	Tent sub. divisions under Capt Hysett proceeded to DIVE COPSE arriving at 4.30 PM Motor transport and 1 motor cyclist proceeded to O.C. X MAC DIVE COPSE	77 H
"	11.8.16		Capt J.S. Flemming R.A.M.C. proceeded to D.H.Q. on appointment as D.A.D.M.S. 35th Division	77 H
"	12.8.16		6. O.R. proceeded to 21 C.C.S. duty. 1 motor cyclist and 6 O.R. Telegraphists on duty met O.C. X MAC DIVE COPSE attached to do motor dental work under O.C. M.D.S. DIVE COPSE	77 H
"	13.8.16		6. O.R. Telegraphists proceeded to duty with 19th I.F. N.T. Lieut D. Kennedy proceeded to report	77 H
"	14.8.16		Nothing to report	77 H
"	15.8.16		Bearer sub-divisions proceeded to HAPPY VALLEY arriving at 6.30 PM Lieut D. J. M. Lyon proceeded for duty with 25th MAN REGT	77 H
HAPPY VALLEY	16.8.16		Nothing to report	77 H
"	17.8.16		Lieut A. C. Agne rejoined unit	77 H
"	18.5.16		Capt D Malcolm posted to 106 Field Ambulance Tent sub-divisions opened Bearer sub-division in HAPPY VALLEY	77 H
"	19.8.16		Field Ambulance proceeded from HAPPY VALLEY and took over A.D.S. WEST PERONNE	77 H
"	20.8.16	7.30 AM	BILLON FARM and dug out at BROMFAY FARM by 10 A.M. Incl 1 motor forwarded to TALUS BOISE and took over dressing station from 142 Field Amb	77 H

1875 Wt. W593/826 1,000,000 4/15 J.B.C. & A. A.D.S.S./Forms/C. 2118.

WAR DIARY or INTELLIGENCE SUMMARY

Army Form C. 2118

(Erase heading not required.)

Place	Date	Hour	Summary of Events and Information	Remarks and references to Appendices
BILLON FARM	20/8/16		1 motor Cyclist sent 6 men reported from O.C. ½ MAC DIVE COPSE	47 H
"	21/8/16		Nothing to report	47 H
"	22/8/16	4.30 AM	Lieut Mackenzie, Lieut Martin, 5 I.O.R. proceeded to CASEMENT TRENCH to relieve	47 H
"	23/8/16		Capt D. & Pendlebury R.A.M.C. posted to 105th Fld Amb for duty	47 H
"	24/8/16		Nothing to report	47 H
"	25/8/16 10AM		Capt Glendy, Lieut Dunne, 5 I.O.R. proceeded to CASEMENT TRENCH to relieve	47 H
"	26/8/16 3 P.M.		Field Ambulance proceeded to CITADE L — arrived at 6 P.M.	47 H
CITADEL	27/8/16		Capt D. & Pendlebury attached on M.O. ½. 33rd M.A. Regt	47 H
"			Lieut D. & Ychel R.A.M.C. posted to 105th Fld Amb	47 H
"			3 R.C.O.R. and 3 men reinforced party from O.C. MDS DIVE COPSE	47 H
"			More Turkic front reinforced from O.C. ½ M.A.C.	47 H
"	28/8/16		Nothing to report	47 H
"	29/8/16		6. O.R. Casualty for duty	47 H
"		10.30 AM	Horse transport under Lieut Mr Open marched with Transport of 144th Bgde T.ALLONVILLE to CANDAS arriving at 6.30 P.M.	47 H
"	30/8/16 19 AM		Horse transport Continued journey to CANDAS	47 H
"		12 noon	Field Ambulance marched to HEILLY and entrained at 6 P.M. detrained at CANDAS at 12	47 H
CANDAS	31/8/16 6.30 AM		Field Ambulance moved to LE SOUICH arriving 1 P.M.	47 H

47 Hegarty
Capt R.A.M.C.
for O.C. 106th Field Ambulance R.A.M.C.

Confidential.

140/171

35 lbs O.D.

Sept 1st 1916

War Diary.

105th Field Ambulance. R.A.M.C.

1st Sept 1916 to 30th Sept 1916. Inclusive.

MEDICAL

Volume VIII.

COMMITTEE FOR THE
MEDICAL HISTORY OF THE WAR
Date —9 DEC. 1916

Original Reply

WAR DIARY
or
INTELLIGENCE SUMMARY
(Erase heading not required.)

Army Form C. 2118

108th FIELD AMBULANCE

Place	Date	Hour	Summary of Events and Information	Remarks and references to Appendices
LE SOUICH	1.9.16		Nothing to report	4FH
"	2.9.16	10 AM	Field Ambulance proceeded to LIGNEREUIL arriving at 1.45 P.M.	4FH
LIGNEREUIL	3.9.16	8 AM	Capt D Mackay. 50 OR proceeded to LOUEZ and took over Divisional Laundry from 64th Fld. Amb.	4FH
"	4.9.16	11 AM	3 Motor Ambulance Cars proceeded to A.D.S. ECOLE NORMALE ARRAS for duty. Capt M J Bowles RAMC posted to 106th Fld. Amb.	4FH
"	5.9.16		2 NCO's and 4 men returned from No 2; 1 & 5 2 NCO's and 4 men returning from M.D.S. DIVE COPSE	4FH
"	6.9.16		A Thurgood to report. Private Todd awarded military medal for bravery in the field by VII Corps Commander.	HMR
"	7.9.16		Nothing to report	HMR
"	8.9.16		Lieut-Col Richard returned to duty from No 15 C.C.S.	HMR
"	9.9.16		Nothing to report	HMR
"	10.9.16		Nothing to report	HMR
"	11.9.16		Took over patients and hospital sheds at the Chateau from No 64 Fd Amb	HMR
"	12.9.16		64th Field Ambulance marched out and took over remainder of site occupied by 64th Fd Amb. including Chateau with School of Instruction, billets, horse lines etc etc	HMR
"	13.9.16		Six men proceeded to MANIN, under instructions from VI Corps to assist Town Major in Sanitary work. These being no Town Major. Six men returned	HMR

WAR DIARY
or
INTELLIGENCE SUMMARY
(Erase heading not required.)

Army Form C. 2118

105th FIELD AMBULANCE

Place	Date	Hour	Summary of Events and Information	Remarks and references to Appendices
LIGNEREUIL	14.9.16		Capt. Cassels RAMC detailed for duty as M.O. 15th L Bde RFA relieving Capt MacKenzie ordered to report for duty with 105th Fd Amb.	JMR
"	15.9.16		Nothing to report	JMR
"	16.9.16		Field Ambulance inspected by Col. H.N. Thompson D.D.M.S. I Corps.	JMR
"	17.9.16		Nothing to report.	JMR
"	18.9.16		Six men ordered to proceed daily to MAHIN, to report to Town Major for Sanitary duties.	JMR
"	19.9.16		Nothing to report.	JMR
"	20.9.16		Nothing to report.	JMR
"	21.9.16		Nothing to report.	JMR
"	22.9.16		In accordance with instructions from D.D.M.S. I Corps patients in hospital gradually evacuated until not more than 20 remain. Lieut Q.M. Tyson proceeded to England on leave of absence.	JMR
"	23.9.16		Nothing to report.	JMR
"	24.9.16		Acting upon instructions by A.D.M.S. 35th Div. Capt. MacKenzie ordered to take over charge of Bath Laundry at LOUEZ vice Capt. Macaulay ordered return to 105th Fd. Amb.	

Army Form C. 2118

WAR DIARY
or
INTELLIGENCE SUMMARY
(Erase heading not required.)

105th FIELD AMBULANCE

Place	Date	Hour	Summary of Events and Information	Remarks and references to Appendices
LIGNEREUIL	24.9.16		Lieut. Morton proceeded to report to C.R.E. 33rd Div. for duty in relief of Lieut. Parkinson. Rame while on leave.	J.M.R.
"	25.9.16		Capt. Mackenzie returned. Capt. Macaulay as O/C Baths & Laundry at LOUEZ. Capt. Macaulay returned to Head Quarters 105 Fd. Amb. Lieut. Morton detailed as M.O. to C.R.E. 33rd Divn during absence on leave of Lieut. Parkinson.	J.M.R. J.M.R.
"	26.9.16		Capt. Macaulay proceeded to IZEL-LES-HAMEAU to see sick of H Coys Gelwt during absence on leave of Capt. Barrs.	J.M.R. J.M.R.
"	27.9.16		Lieut. McCafer detailed M.O. 1/15 D.L.I. during absence on leave of Capt. Barrs.	J.M.R.
"	28.9.16		Nothing to report.	J.M.R.

Army Form C. 2118

WAR DIARY
or
INTELLIGENCE SUMMARY
(Erase heading not required.)

105th FIELD AMBULANCE

Place	Date	Hour	Summary of Events and Information	Remarks and references to Appendices
LIGNEREUIL	29.9.16		Nothing to report.	JMR
"	30.9.16		Letter received from A.D.M.S. asking for names of officers desirous of an exchange to HAVRE, names of Capt. Macaulay and Capt. Mackenzie submitted.	JMR

J M Richard
Lt Col R.A.M.C.
O.C. 105 Field Ambulance

Confidential.

War Diary.

of

105th Field Ambulance, R.A.M.C.

From

1st October. 1916.

to

31st October. 1916.

Inclusive.

Volume IX.   (Original).

140/1817

35th Div.

Oct. 1916

Army Form C. 2118

WAR DIARY
or
INTELLIGENCE SUMMARY
(Erase heading not required.)

105th FIELD AMBULANCE

Place	Date	Hour	Summary of Events and Information	Remarks and references to Appendices
LIGNEREUIL	1.10.16		Nothing to report.	M.R.
"	2.10.16		Field Ambulance inspected by A.D.S. 35th Division.	M.R.
"	3.10.16		Capt. T. Archer R.A.M.C. posted to 105th Fd Amb.	
"			Capt. Dickin detailed to visit Corps Cyclists at IZEL-LES-HAMEAU.	M.R.
"	4.10.16		Capt. D. Macaulay proceeded to HAVRE on duty and was struck off the strength.	M.R.
"			Lieut. Tyson returned from leave.	
"	5.10.16		Nothing to report.	M.R.
"	6.10.16		Nothing to report.	M.R.
"	7.10.16		Nothing to report.	M.R.
"	8.10.16		Nothing to report.	M.R.
"	9.10.16		Capt. Archer detailed for duty as M.O. Divisional Bombing School at HAUTEVILLE. Lieut. Browne proceeded to IZEL to see sick of VI Corps Cyclists.	M.R.
"	10.10.16		Capt. Hegarty and Lieut. McGibb, one N.C.O and twelve men detailed to be in readiness to proceed to No.19. C.C.S at DOULLENS.	M.R.
"			Capt. Hegarty proceeded to IZEL to see sick of VI Corps Cyclists.	M.R.
"	11.10.16		Capt. Hegarty proceeded to IZEL.	M.R.

WAR DIARY
or
INTELLIGENCE SUMMARY
(Erase heading not required.)

105th FIELD AMBULANCE

Army Form C. 2118

Place	Date	Hour	Summary of Events and Information	Remarks and references to Appendices
LIGNEREUIL	12.10.16		Capt. Hegarty proceeded to 12FA to see sick of VI Corps Cyclists. Lieut. Morton returned from duty with C.R.E. 35th Division.	JWR
"	13.10.16		Lieut. Morton proceeded to 12FA. Lieut. Dr Capes returned from duty with 19th D.L.I.	JWR
"	14.10.16		Lieut. Morton proceeded to 12FA. Field Ambulance visited by A.D.M.S. 35th Division.	JWR
"	15.10.16		1st Line transport inspected by the A.A. & Q.M.G. 35th Division at 3.30 p.m.	JWR
"	16.10.16		Acting under instructions from A.D.M.S. 35th Divn & Capt. Archer ordered to proceed to LOUEZ to take over charge of Divisional Bath & Laundry. Capt. McKenzie on relief by Capt. Archer proceeded to HAUTEVILLE and assumed duty of M.O./c Bon. Boys' School. Notified by A.D.M.S. 35th Division that arrangement had been made that Sick of VI Corps Cyclists would be seen by an officer of the 2nd Echelon. Sergeant Shelton proceeded to IIIrd Army School of Cookery for course of instruction from 16/10/16 to 28/10/16.	JWR
"	17.10.16		Work of fitting up new shed as a ward & converting the other shed into a reserve clean room to hold D. fifty beds, mattresses & blankets obtained from Red Cross.	JWR

1875 Wt. W593/826 1,000,000 4/15 I.B.C. & A. A.D.S.S./Forms/C.2118.

WAR DIARY
or
INTELLIGENCE SUMMARY
(Erase heading not required.)

105th FIELD AMBULANCE

Army Form C. 2118

Place	Date	Hour	Summary of Events and Information	Remarks and references to Appendices
LIGNEREUIL	18.10.16		Nothing to report.	J.M.R.
"	19.10.16		8 men proceeded for duty with 203rd Fd. Coy. R.E.	J.M.R.
"	20.10.16		Revd. Kenton proceeded to Divl. Bomb School Hauteville, relieves Capt: Mackenzie who is transferred to 14th Division for duty. Capt: Grant posted 105 Fd. Amb. transferred from 114 F. Division.	J.M.R.
"	21.10.16		Sergt. Anderson & 12 men proceeded to Dusans to help in harvest work.	J.M.R.
"	22.10.16		Corpl. Knight proceeded to Hauteville to undergo a course of instruction at Divisional Gas School.	J.M.R.
"	23.10.16		Capt. Hegarty proceeded to Hauteville to relieve Capt Grant as 2nd i/c School. Latter officer returns to H.Qrs 105 Fd. Amb.	J.M.R.
"	24.10.16		Capt. in Capt. Capt. Grant 1 NCO & 12 men proceeded to No 19 C.C.S. for duty.	J.M.R.
"	25.10.16		Nothing to report.	
"	26.10.16		" "	
"	27.10.16		" "	
"	28.10.16		" "	
"	29.10.16		" "	
"	30.10.16		" "	
"	31.10.16		Capt. Locker appointed S.A.D.A.S. 30th Division, and struck off strength.	J.M.R.

A.H. Richard. Lieut Colonel.
O.C. 105 Field Ambulance

Confidential.

War Diary

of

105th Field Ambulance. R.A.M.C.

From

1st November 1916.

to

30th November. 1916.

Inclusive.

Volume X.   Original

Army Form C. 2118

WAR DIARY
or
INTELLIGENCE SUMMARY
(Erase heading not required.)

105th FIELD AMBULANCE

Instructions regarding War Diaries and Intelligence Summaries are contained in F. S. Regs., Part II. and the Staff Manual respectively. Title Pages will be prepared in manuscript.

Place	Date	Hour	Summary of Events and Information	Remarks and references to Appendices
LIGNEREUIL	1.11.16		Lieut. Donovan granted leave from 1.11.16 to 11.11.16	J.M.R.
"	2.11.16		Nothing to report.	J.M.R.
"	3.11.16		Nothing to report.	J.M.R.
"	4.11.16		School of Instruction opened at LIGNEREUIL. Lectures from II Corps. Major Tyndale and Lieut Walker. 10 Officers and 65 O.R. reported and were taken on ration strength.	J.M.R.
"	5.11.16		Eight men returned from 203rd Fld. Coy. R.E. Nothing to report.	J.M.R. J.M.R.
"	6.11.16		Lieut. L. M. MORTON R.A.M.C. proceeded to England on expiry of contract and was struck off strength of unit. Capt. R. A. MORELL 25th Fd. Amb. temporarily attached to 105th Fd. Amb. to assist in School of Instruction.	J.M.R. J.M.R.
"	7.11.16		Stretcher Bearers and Sanitary Personnel under instruction returned to their units. No 63700 Pte Beard Tony J. proceeded to TREVIN CAPELLE for duty at the rest camp.	J.M.R. J.M.R.

Army Form C. 2118

WAR DIARY
or
INTELLIGENCE SUMMARY
(Erase heading not required.)

105th FIELD AMBULANCE.

Place	Date	Hour	Summary of Events and Information	Remarks and references to Appendices
LIGNEREUIL	8.11.16		No 63641 Pte Clendon J.K. attached to 106th Inf. Bgde to act as instructor in laundry work.	JMR
"	9.11.16		Capt. D.J. A. Eyles, Capt. J.M. Grant and eleven O.R. returned from duty at No 19 C.C.S. Doullens.	JMR
"	10.11.16		Course at School of Instruction completed. Officers and NCOs returned to their units.	JMR
"	11.11.16		Nothing to report.	JMR
"	12.11.16		Nothing to report.	JMR
"	13.11.16		Two days course of massage commenced for men acting as Medical Officers orderly & those in W Corps. Course of Instruction for Officers, Nt. Comd. NCOs, Stretcher Bearers and Sanitary Personal commenced.	JMR
"	14.11.16		Massage course completed. Under instructions from A.D.M.S 35th Divi. Accommodation at LIGNEREUIL expanded to form a Divisional Rest Station.	JMR

Army Form C. 2118

WAR DIARY
or
INTELLIGENCE SUMMARY
(Erase heading not required.)

105 FIELD AMBULANCE.

Place	Date	Hour	Summary of Events and Information	Remarks and references to Appendices
LIGNEREUIL	15.11.16		Capt. C.V. Cornish posted to 105th Field Ambulance, a reinforcement	App.
"	16.11.16		Massage course commenced.	App.
"	17.11.16		Massage course completed. Course for Officers, NCOs, Stretcher Bearers and Sanitary personnel completed. Capt. Howell 28-2 Fd Amb. returned to his unit.	App.
"	18.11.16		Lieut. O.G. Donovan struck off strength of unit under instruction for A.D.M.S. contract expired.	App.
"	19.11.16		Nothing to report.	App.
"	20.11.16		Capt. Cornish proceeded to IIIrd Army School for course of instruction in "Gas".	App.
"	21.11.16		Nothing to report.	App.
"	22.11.16		Lieut. A.R. Hill RAMC posted to 105th Fd A.L. a reinforcement	App.
"	23.11.16		Nothing to report.	App.
"	24.11.16		Nothing to report.	App.

WAR DIARY or **INTELLIGENCE SUMMARY**
(Erase heading not required.)

Army Form C. 2118

105 H/H Field Ambulance

Place	Date	Hour	Summary of Events and Information	Remarks and references to Appendices
LIGNEREUIL	25.11.16		Capt. Cornish returned from Course of Instruction at 1st Army School	J.F.R
"	26.11.16		Capt. Cornish detailed O/C wards inside Chateau, Lieut Hill O/C wards outside. Unit visited by A.D.M.S.	J.M.R
"	27.11.16		Nothing to report.	
"	28.11.16		Nothing to report.	
"	29.11.16		Sergt. Chatham and Pte Lanyard proceeded on leave	J.F.R
"	30.11.16		Nothing to report.	J.F.R

J.H.Bigham.
Lieut. Col. R.a.m.C.
O.C. 105 H Field Ambulance.

Confidential.

War Diary

of

105th Field Ambulance.

From

1st December 1916.

to

31st December 1916.

Inclusive.

Volume XI   Original.

WAR DIARY or INTELLIGENCE SUMMARY

105th FIELD AMBULANCE

Army Form C. 2118

Place	Date	Hour	Summary of Events and Information	Remarks and references to Appendices
LIGNEREUIL	DEC. 1st		Notified verbally by D.D.M.S. III Corps that a Course of Instruction would commence on Dec. 4th.	J.P.R.
"	" 2nd		Informed by telephone from III Corps that proposed course of instruction is cancelled owing to movement of Divisions.	J.P.R.
"	" 3rd		Lieut. A. R. HILL detailed to see sick of Nos. 3 & 4 Coy. 35th Divisional Train daily commencing 4.12.16. Capt. T.F. HEGARTY returned from Div'l Bombing School, Hautville.	
"	" 4th		Advance party and quarter master of 107th Field Ambulance arrived to take over.	J.P.R.
"	" 5 9.30am		Field Ambulance proceeded from LIGNEREUIL to MAIZIERES arriving at 11.45am. and took over site from South African Field Ambulance, consisting of one small farm used as a hospital & capable of accommodating 10 patients. Baths of spray type, 12 sprays supplied with hot water from a "Blanc Bain". Laundry and drying rooms, Q.M. stores, cookhouse etc. Men accommodated in billets, horses in barns & sheds, wagons parked on a piece of arable land & motor ambulances parked at side of road. Capt. Cormack detailed as officer in charge of baths & laundry at Souty.	J.P.R.

WAR DIARY or INTELLIGENCE SUMMARY

Army Form C. 2118

105th FIELD AMBULANCE.

Place	Date	Hour	Summary of Events and Information	Remarks and references to Appendices
MAZIERES	Dec. 6th		In order to increase accommodation for patients, a shed in the yard of an estaminet was taken over. Capable of taking six patients, a large barn containing wheat & hay belonging to the Maire was selected & arrangements made to have it shifted as soon as possible.	J.H.R.
"	" 7th		Capt. Hegarty detailed as M.C. Hospital, Baths & Laundry.	J.H.R.
"	" 8th		One motor ambulance detailed to visit AVERDOINGT, LIGNY, and FOUFFLIN -RICAMETZ daily to collect sick, & one motor ambulance to visit MAISNIL-ST POL, GOUY-EN-TERNOIS and MAGNICOURT.	J.H.R.
"	" 9th		Nothing to report.	J.H.R.
"	" 9th		Nothing to report.	
"	" 9th		No 54888 Cpl. Northwood detailed to attend course of instruction at III Army School of Cookery from 9.12.16 to 22.12.16.	J.H.R.
"	" 10th		No 66989 Cpl. Featherstone proceeded to attend Course of instruction at III Corps School LIGNEREUIL.	J.H.R.
"	" 11th		Nothing to report.	J.H.R.
"	" 12th		Nothing to report.	J.H.R.

WAR DIARY or INTELLIGENCE SUMMARY

Army Form C. 2118

105th FIELD AMBULANCE.

Place	Date	Hour	Summary of Events and Information	Remarks and references to Appendices
MAIZIERES	Dec. 13th		Capt. N.B. GRAHAM. R.A.M.C. posted to 105th Fd. Amb. as a/s reinforcement.	J.H.R.
"	" 14th		Capt. Graham detailed to take over duties of O/c Hospital, Beds. & Laundry. Nothing to report.	J.H.R.
"	" 15th			J.H.R.
"	" 16th		Capt. T.F. HEGARTY R.A.M.C. granted leave from 16 — 27.12.16.	J.H.R.
"			Capt. Pray C. detailed to proceed daily to Villers Sir Simon to see sick of 35th Div. Supply Column & Lieut. A.R. Hill proceeded to Inisons to take over duty of officer i/c working party engaged in road construction.	
"	" 17th		Capt. Grant detailed to see sick of nos 3+4 Co. 35th Div. Train vice Lieut. Hill. Capt. Featherstone returned from course of instruction at sig. general.	J.H.R.
"	18th		Work of improving hutlets and hut and tent generally hampered by difficulty of obtaining material, particularly wood. Sand, ballast and cement has been resorted to in order to make a floor for Laundry.	J.H.R.

WAR DIARY or INTELLIGENCE SUMMARY

Army Form C. 2118

105th FIELD AMBULANCE

Place	Date	Hour	Summary of Events and Information	Remarks and references to Appendices
MAZIERES	Dec.18 (cont.)		But there appears to be likelihood of delay in obtaining these materials.	J.M.R.
"	Dec.19		Nothing to report.	J.M.R.
"	"20		Nothing to report.	J.M.R.
"	"21		Capt. D.J.R. Giles R.A.M.C. appointed town major of Mazières as a temporary measure.	J.M.R.
"	"22		Pte Witherell detailed as sanitary orderly to town major. Cpl. Northward returned from 3rd Army School of Cookery.	J.M.R.
"	"23	10 A.M.	Gas lecture by Lieut. Hume Div'l. Gas Officer to Officers, W.O.s & Senior N.C.O.s on Utility & for respirators.	J.M.R.
"	"24		Nothing to report. Dvr. Wallace & Harrower A.S.C. charged with being absent from billet at 9 p.m. on 22.12.16 and each awarded 14 days F.P. No. 2. Dvr. Saunders & Thompson, A.S.C. charged with being drunk and absenting to strike a N.C.O. Both cases remanded for a summary of	J.M.R.

WAR DIARY
or
INTELLIGENCE SUMMARY

Army Form C. 2118

105th FIELD AMBULANCE.

Place	Date	Hour	Summary of Events and Information	Remarks and references to Appendices
MAIZIERES	Dec 23rd		Capt. M Clyse detached to take summary of evidence in case of Dr Snowden & Dr Thompson.	
"	"24th		Nothing to report.	J.M.R.
"	"25th		Nothing to report.	J.M.R.
"	"26th		Drs Snowden & Thompson charged under Sect. 15 A.A. & Sect. 8(2) A.A. Charge sheets in duplicate, summary of evidence, list of witnesses for the Prosecution and application for a Field General Court Martial forwarded to A.D.M.S. 35th Division.	
"	"27th		Nothing to report.	J.M.R.
"	"28th		Nothing to report.	J.M.R.
"	"29th		Capt. Grant Ramé granted leave from 29.12.16 to 12.1.17, 14 days on expiry of contract.	J.M.R.
"	"30th		Nothing to report.	
"	"31st		Nothing to report.	

J M Richard
Lieut. Col. Ramé
O.C. 105 Field Ambulance.

— Confidential —

— War Diary —

— 105th Field Ambulance —

From

— 1st January 1917 —

to

— 31st January 1917 —

Inclusive.

Volume XII   Original.

WAR DIARY or INTELLIGENCE SUMMARY

Army Form C. 2118

105th FIELD AMBULANCE

Place	Date	Hour	Summary of Events and Information	Remarks and references to Appendices
MAILLY MAILLET RES.	1.1.17		Pte Watson F. rejoined unit and taken on strength; released from prison on suspension of sentence. Having served half the sentence of one year I.H.L. (authority A.G. GHQ B/R 28 a/26.12.16. Inspection of unit by A.D.M.S. 35th Division.	JMR
"	2.1.17		Supply O.R. fitted with Box Respirators. Officers posted to sections on re-arrangement, as follows:- A. 2/Lt Richard, Capt. Cornish (i/c Tent Sub-div), Capt Grant (i/c Bearer S.D.) B. Capt Hegarty, Lieut. Hill (i/c Bearer S.D.) Lieut Totten (i/c Tent S.D.) C. Capt Graham (i/c Bearer S.D.) Capt McAfee (i/c Tent S.D.). Capt Hegarty detailed o/c Motor Transport	JMR
"	3.1.17		50 O.R. fitted with Box Respirators. Capt Graham detailed to duty with R.E. 35th Divn in relief of Capt Parkinson. Capt Cornish and 42 O.R. returned from Divn Bath & Laundry Conv.	JMR
"	4.1.17		Capt. Cornish detailed O/c Bath and Laundry. Capt Hegarty detailed to take over Hospital Barns.	JMR
"	5.1.17		6 O.R. returned from Divn Bath & Laundry Conv.	JMR
"	6.1.17		F.G.C.M. assembled at Hd Qrs 104th Machine Gun Co. for trial of 1/725956 Dr Swerston J.E. & 7/83291 Dr Thorburn A. A.S.C. Capt McAfee detailed as officer in attendance.	JMR

WAR DIARY or INTELLIGENCE SUMMARY

Army Form C. 2118

105th FIELD AMBULANCE.

Place	Date	Hour	Summary of Events and Information	Remarks and references to Appendices
MAIZIERES	7.1.17.		Capt. Cornish detailed to visit units in place of Capt. McAfee. Not inspected for A Coy. 9 men returned from Louey.	J.M.R.
"	8.1.17.		Braces drilled in adjustment of Box Respirators by Capt. Cornish.	J.M.R.
"	9.1.17.		Two motor ambulances from 12th Division attached for purpose of collecting sick from 12th Divisional Artillery.	J.M.R.
"	10.1.17.		Sergt. McKnight & L/Cpl Taafe proceeded to VI Corps School of Instruction at Lignereuil to attend course from 11.1.17 to 17.1.17. Ptes Snowden and Thompson A.S.C. Sentenced by F.G.C.M. to two years I.H.L. and Fined £1. on 6.1.17. Sentence confirmed by Brig. Genl. J.W. Sandilands, Condg. 104 Inf. Brigade on 8.1.17 and promulgated by O.C. 105 F.A. on 9.1.17. Orders received to retain prisoners.	J.M.R.
"	11.1.17		Nothing to report.	J.M.R.
"	12.1.17		Pte Duffenden detailed for duty as orderly to O.C. Depot Battn. 33rd-H.Brn-2.	J.M.R.
"	13.1.17.		No 2/150175 Pte Hunter and No 2/139325 Pte Sayers R.A.C. (M.T.) transferred to Div. Supply Column in accordance with instructions to reduce M.T. personnel of 13 as a struck off strength	J.M.R.

Army Form C. 2118

WAR DIARY
or
INTELLIGENCE SUMMARY
(Erase heading not required.)

105th FIELD AMBULANCE.

Instructions regarding War Diaries and Intelligence Summaries are contained in F. S. Regs., Part II. and the Staff Manual respectively. Title Pages will be prepared in manuscript.

Place	Date	Hour	Summary of Events and Information	Remarks and references to Appendices
MAIZIERES	14.1.17		Nothing to report.	J.H.R.
"	15.1.17		Capt. Heafy proceeded for duty as MO 1/c 16th Cheshires in relief of Capt Stewart. Proceeded on leave. Lieut Hollis RAMC (TC) posted to 105th Fd Amb.	J.H.R.
"	16.1.17		Lieut Col Richard proceeded on leave from 16.1.17 to 26.1.17. Capt Hegarty assumed command of 105th Fd Amb.	J.H.R.
"	17.1.17		Lieut Hollis detailed to proceed daily to see sick of units. Capt Upshaw rejoined unit from RE 35th Divn and proceeded for duty with 1/6th Royal Scotts in relief of Lieut F. Crean. Latter then posted to 105th Fd Amb. As a temporary measure pending receipt of orders to proceed to the base.	J.H.R.
"	18.1.17		Lieut Crean proceeded to the base under instructions from A.D.M.S. 35th Divn. Testing of box respirators with tear gas carried out.	J.H.R.
"	19.1.17		Sentences awarded to Dr Lunsden and Pt Thompson A.S.C. by L.G.O.C. Commuted in each case to two months 2 P. No. 1. by Army Commander. Third Army. (Authority 3rd Army S.A.L. 11/5609 dated 17.1.17.	J.H.R.
"	20.1.17		Dr Lunsden and Pt Thompson A.S.C. committed to charge of A.P.M. 35th Divn to undergo sentences awarded.	J.H.R.

Army Form C. 2118

WAR DIARY
or
INTELLIGENCE SUMMARY
(Erase heading not required.)

105 FIELD AMBULANCE

Instructions regarding War Diaries and Intelligence Summaries are contained in F.S. Regs., Part II. and the Staff Manual respectively. Title Pages will be prepared in manuscript.

Place	Date	Hour	Summary of Events and Information	Remarks and references to Appendices
MAIZIERES	20.1.17		No 43208 L/h. Sgt. Burrows W. R and C reduced to the ranks for inefficiency under Sect. 183(2) A.A. (Authority VI Corps A 2981 dated 17.1.17.	J.M.R.
"	21.1.17		7/30199 Dr Skinner J. A.S.C. detailed to attend Cooking Class Assembling at 33rd Div.l School from 21.1.17 to 4.2.17.	J.M.R.
"	22.1.17		Nothing to report.	J.M.R.
"	23.1.17		Lecture for B Section by Capt. T.J. Hegarty.	J.M.R.
"	24.1.17		Capt. J.M. Grant detailed for Infantry duty with 19th Durham Light Infantry in chg of Capt. Bows R and C attending a course of Instruction.	J.M.R.
"	25.1.17		Sergt. Anderson and Eleven men proceeded to ARRAS to continue work on an advanced Dressing Station taking over from a party of 9th Divn.	J.M.R.
"	26.1.17		Nothing to report.	J.M.R.
"	27.1.17		Capt. Grant rejoined unit from duty with 19th Durham Light Infantry.	J.M.R.
"	28.1.17		Lt-Col Richard returned from leave and resumed Command of 105 F.A.	J.M.R.

Army Form C. 2118

WAR DIARY
or
INTELLIGENCE SUMMARY

(Erase heading not required.) 105 FIELD AMBULANCE.

Instructions regarding War Diaries and Intelligence Summaries are contained in F.S. Regs., Part II. and the Staff Manual respectively. Title Pages will be prepared in manuscript.

Place	Date	Hour	Summary of Events and Information	Remarks and references to Appendices
MAIZIERES	29.1.17		Capt M Apes reported out from duty with 16th Cheshires. Sergt Anderson and party of men returned from Arras, later return of later-party cancelled by D.D.M.S. and then under instructions from D.D.M.S.	J.H.R.
"	30.1.17		Under instructions from A.D.M.S. 35th Division Capt. Bagott Rame (S.R.) is posted to 105th Fd. Amb. transferred from 106th Fd. Amb. Lieut. Millar Rame proceeded for duty with 106th Fd. Amb. transferred from 105 Fd. Amb.	J.H.R.
"	31.1.17		Scabies cases transferred from 106th Fd. Amb. on 30.1.17 accommodated in large barn originally in use as a hospital. Arrangements for conducting laundry into bath house for these cases completed. Serbian stand for disinfection of clothing erected near drying room. Visit of D.D.M.S. IIIrd Army to inspect bathing arrangements, cancelled.	J.H.R.

J H Rigbard
Lieut. Col. R.a.m.e.
O.C. 105th Field Ambulance.

Confidential.

War Diary

of

105th Field Ambulance R.A.M.C.

From

1st February 1917.

to

28th February 1917

Inclusive.

Volume XIII   Original

Army Form C. 2118

WAR DIARY
or
INTELLIGENCE SUMMARY
(Erase heading not required.)

105th FIELD AMBULANCE

Place	Date	Hour	Summary of Events and Information	Remarks and references to Appendices
MARIZIERES	1.2.17		Capt. Bazett detailed to see be of units visited by Lieut. Killas.	J.M.R.
"	2.2.17		Nothing to report.	J.M.R.
"	3.2.17		Verbal intimation received with reference to move of the Division to new area.	J.M.R.
"	4.2.17		Nothing to report.	J.M.R.
"	5.2.17		Ambulance Car of 12th Division, attached 105th Fd. Amb. for purpose of collecting sick from Artillery units, returned to 38th Fd. Amb. Captn. H.C. Bazett posted to C section as Officer i/c Bearer Subdivision vice Son. Lieut. attached for the move and taken on ration strength.	J.M.R.
"	6.2.17	10 P.M.	105th Fd. Amb proceeded to LIGNY-SUR-CANCHE arriving at 3.15 p.m. Unit attached to and rationed by 106th Inf. Brigade for move to new area. Horse ambulances detailed to march in rear of 17th Royal Scots, 17th West Yorks and 19th D.L.I. orderly in charge of each wagon instructed to take names of men carried during march, for purpose of return to A.D.M.S. Motor transport proceeded independently after collection & disposal of sick under orders of Capt. Hegarty. One motor Ambulance attached for duty with 106th Bde. H.Qrs. during move.	J.M.R.

WAR DIARY
or
INTELLIGENCE SUMMARY
(Erase heading not required.)

105th FIELD AMBULANCE

Army Form C. 2118

Place	Date	Hour	Summary of Events and Information	Remarks and references to Appendices
LIGNY SUR CANCHE	7.2.17	8 p.m.	105th Fd. Amb. proceeded to OCCOCHES arriving at 12.30 a.m. Horse Ambulances detailed to march as one 6th Motor transport, after collection of sick preceding independently, under Capt. Hegarty.	J.W.R.
OCCOCHES	8.2.17	10.19 p.m.	105th Fd. Amb. proceeded to VIGNACOURT arriving at 4 p.m. Brigade moved as a whole. Horse Ambulances marched with Fd. Amb. Brigade. Ambulance detailed to collect sick from 17th Royal Scots. One motor and one to collect from 17th West Yorks and 18th H.L.I. Capt. Grant detailed for temporary duty with 19th D.L.I. during absence on leave of Capt. Cassels.	J.W.R.
VIGNACOURT	9.2.17		Capt. Cornish granted leave from 9.2.17 to 19.2.17. Capt. Bazett detailed as officer i/c hospital. E.F.C. house attached to het factory taken over as hospital, providing accommodation for thirty patients.	J.W.R.
"	10.2.17	10 a.m.	Bearer subdivisions of all Fd. Ambs. inspected by A.D.M.S. 35th Division. A.D.M.S. stressed the desire that every opportunity should be taken	J.W.R.

WAR DIARY
or
INTELLIGENCE SUMMARY
(Erase heading not required.) 105 FIELD AMBULANCE.

Army Form C. 2118

Place	Date	Hour	Summary of Events and Information	Remarks and references to Appendices
VIGNACOURT	10.2.17	(cont.)	of training all ranks and particularly bearers during the short stay in the present area.	J.M.R.
"	11.2.17	2.30 pm	Bearer Subdivisions proceeded for route march under Lieut. Hill.	J.M.R.
"	12.2.17	10 A.M.	Horse transport of Field Amb. paraded with 1st line transport of 106th Inf. Brigade for inspection by A.D. & D.M.S. 35th Division.	J.M.R.
"	"	2 pm	Bearers instructed in carriage of wounded on stretchers and in contents of surgical haversacks by Capt. Bazell.	
"	13.2.17	2 pm	Bearer Subdivisions proceeded for route march under charge of Lieuts. Hill and Tobin.	J.M.R.
"	14.2.17	2 pm	Bearer Subdivisions instructed by Capt. Bazell. Lieut. Totin proceeded for temporary duty with King Edward's Horse.	J.M.R.

Army Form C. 2118

WAR DIARY
or
INTELLIGENCE SUMMARY
(Erase heading not required.)

105th FIELD AMBULANCE

Place	Date	Hour	Summary of Events and Information	Remarks and references to Appendices
VIGNACOURT	15.2.17.		Nothing to report.	G.M.R.
"	16.2.17.		No 9145 S/Sergeant MAY. A. posted to 105 H Fd Amb. as a reinforcement.	G.M.R.
"	17.2.17.		Personnel of Unit subdivisions instructed in contents of Medical & Surgical Panniers & P.T.H.	G.M.R.
"	18.2.17.	7.30 p.m.	Horse transport proceeded to AUBIGNY marching with transport of 106 A.H. Brigade, Capt. McCafer RAMC being in charge. One motor ambulance detailed to 106 H Inf Brigade H.Qrs for use of Staff Captain.	G.M.R.
		9. p.m.	Motor lorry reported arrived, told off for purpose of carrying surplus Blankets, Tarpaulins, utensils and Officers Kit.	
"	19.2.17.	12 noon	Personnel entrained at Vignacourt Station, arrived at MARCELCAVE at 3 p.m. Horse transport marched from AUBIGNY and arrived at MARCELCAVE at 2 p.m.	G.M.R.

WAR DIARY
or
INTELLIGENCE SUMMARY

Army Form C. 2118

105 FIELD AMBULANCE

Place	Date	Hour	Summary of Events and Information	Remarks and references to Appendices
VIGNACOURT	19.2.17	(Cont.)	with transport, under Capt. Hegarty, proceeded to Hangard. 74.	JMR
MARCELCAVE	20.2.17		Lieut. A.R. Hill proceeded for temporary duty with 1st Lancashire Fusiliers. No 68336 Pte Hicks proceeded to MOREUIL as orderly with III Corps Hd. Qrs. and struck off strength.	JMR
"	21.2.17		Proceeded to Hill 75 to ascertain portable site of move of French Field Ambulance.	JMR
"	22.2.17		105th Fd. Amb. moved from MARCELCAVE marching out at 2p.m. Capt. W. Coles, all R.A.M.C. personnel and wagons billeted with French unit at Hill 75. Remain: officers, R.A.M.C. personnel and horses proceeded to LE QUESNEL and billeted there on night of 22.2.17. Two Horse Subdivisions under S/Sergt. Hay Ram C. detached at CAIX on the march and ordered to proceed to ROSIERES and report to O.C. 104 Fd. Amb.	JMR

Army Form C. 2118

WAR DIARY
or
INTELLIGENCE SUMMARY
(Erase heading not required.)

105th FIELD AMBULANCE

Place	Date	Hour	Summary of Events and Information	Remarks and references to Appendices
LE QUESNEL CAMP.	23.2.17.		Capt. H.C. Bazett proceeded to No 7 General Hospital and struck off the strength. Details billetted at Le Quesnel proceeded to the Camp and the site was taken over from the 14th French Fd. A. L. Transport lines allotted to 105th Fd. A. L. being occupied by transport of 14th Kane Fus. Report to that effect sent to A.D.M.S. C.R.E. requested to have one shed numbered in order to increase accommodation. Accommodation available for patients between forty and fifty. By means of bunking with material available locally, accommodation can be provided for eighty patients.	J.M.R.
"	24.2.17.		Transport lines evacuated by 14th R. Fus. and taken over.	J.M.R.
"	25.2.17.		Cpl. Geraghty and four men proceeded for duty at the Baths at CAIX.	J.M.R.

Army Form C. 2118

WAR DIARY
or
INTELLIGENCE SUMMARY
(Erase heading not required.)

105th FIELD AMBULANCE

Instructions regarding War Diaries and Intelligence Summaries are contained in F.S. Regs., Part II. and the Staff Manual respectively. Title Pages will be prepared in manuscript.

Place	Date	Hour	Summary of Events and Information	Remarks and references to Appendices
LE QUESNEL CAMP.	26.2.17		The A.D.M.S. IV Corps visited the unit and inspected the site occupied by the F.Amb.	Appx.
"	27.2.17		Nothing to report.	Appx.
"	28.2.17		Capt. Grant rejoined from temporary duty with 154 Bde. R.F.A. Capt. Cornish returned from leave. Lieut. Hill rejoined from temporary duty with 15th Lanc. Fusiliers.	Appx.
"	29.2.17		Accommodation for sick increased to take in about a hundred patients.	

G.M. Richard.
Lieut. Colonel. R.a.m.C
O.C. 105th Field Ambulance.

Confidential.

Vol 14

War Diary

of

105th Field Ambulance. R.A.M.C.

From

1st March 1917.

to

31st March 1917.

Inclusive.

Volume XIV

Original.

35th Div.

Mar 1917

WAR DIARY
or
INTELLIGENCE SUMMARY

Army Form C. 2118

105th FIELD AMBULANCE

Place	Date	Hour	Summary of Events and Information	Remarks and references to Appendices
LE QUESNEL CAMP.	1.3.17.		Privates Eckersley F., Boise R. and Mulligan R.T. proceeded to Transportation Troops Depôt Boulogne for transfer to R.E. (Railway Construction Corps) and are struck off the Strength. Capt. Cornish detailed to take charge of hospital with view of cases of Trench Feet. Lieut. Peel detailed to take charge of latter. Capt. Grant detailed O/c Sanitation. The D.M.S. IV Army accompanied by D.D.M.S. III Corps visited tent.	JHP
"	2.3.17		Nothing to report.	JHP
"	3.3.17		Nothing to report.	JHP
"	4.3.17		Capt. C.V. Ernest Ranc detailed as M.O/c 23rd Manchester Regt vice Capt. Adam posted to 105th Fd Amb. Lieut. E.S. Bull Rome (Transport) attached to IV Corps H.Q.) posted to 105th Fd A.t. as from 26.2.17. Capt. Adam detailed as M. O/c Depot Battn and Divisional Schools.	JHP
"	6.3.17.		Nothing to report.	JHP

WAR DIARY
or
INTELLIGENCE SUMMARY
(Erase heading not required.)

Army Form C. 2118

105th FIELD AMBULANCE

Place	Date	Hour	Summary of Events and Information	Remarks and references to Appendices
LE QUESNEL CAMP	5.3.17		Unit visited by M.G.C. 35th Division.	J.M.R.
"	6.3.17		Lieut. Titini returned for duty with King Edward's Horse.	J.M.R.
"	7.3.17		Inspection by G.O.C. IV Corps. Accompanied by D.D.M.S. No 43769 Pte Watson J. Ramc tried by F.G.C.M. Charge. When on active service Drunkenness. Finding Guilty. Sentence Fined #1 and 2 years I.H.L. Confirmed by Brig. Gen. R.W. Chamberlin Comdg. 105th Inf. Brigade. Promulgated at 2 p.m.	J.M.R.
"	8.3.17		Nothing to report.	J.M.R.
"	10.3.17		Nothing to report.	J.M.R.
"	11.3.17		Lieut. Titini proceeded to duty with 15th Sherwood Foresters in relief of Capt. J.H. Miller posted to 105th Bat Inf. No 68107 of Pte Collis F.W. proceeded to 33rd Divisional School to attend 6 Cookery Class.	J.M.R.
"	12.3.17		Capt. Miller reported for duty with Fd. Amb.	J.M.R.

WAR DIARY
or
INTELLIGENCE SUMMARY
(Erase heading not required.)

Army Form C. 2118

Instructions regarding War Diaries and Intelligence Summaries are contained in F. S. Regs., Part II. and the Staff Manual respectively. Title Pages will be prepared in manuscript.

Place	Date	Hour	Summary of Events and Information	Remarks and references to Appendices
LEQUESNEL (AMP)	13.3.17.		Nothing to report.	JMR
"	14.3.17		3 NCOs and 23 men returned from duty with 107th & 3rd Cavd.	JMR
"	15.3.17.		Capt. Miller posted to C Section. Officer i/c Bearer Subdivision. Lieut. A.S. Bull posted to A Section. Tpt Subdivision.	JMR
"	16.3.17.		Medical Board assembled to examine A.S/Sgt Major Parker J.R. A.S.C. as to his physical fitness for a permanent commission in the Regular Army. President Capt. Hegarty R.A.M.C. Members Capt 15 H/gts & Capt Miller R.A.M.C. Lieut. Bull granted leave from 16.3.17 to 26.3.17. Military Medal awarded to 80996 Pte J.W. Bowers, 64484 Pte H. Barlow and Bar to Military Medal to 63916 Pte Tonlol. by Corps Commander and presented by ADMS 25th Division.	JMR JMR
"	17.3.17.		Nothing to report.	JMR
"	18.3.17.		C Section complete with transport reported at ADMS office at 8 A.M. Capt. Rogers O/c Section and Capt Miller O/c Bearer Subdivision.	JMR

WAR DIARY
or
INTELLIGENCE SUMMARY
(Erase heading not required.)

Army Form C. 2118

Place	Date	Hour	Summary of Events and Information	Remarks and references to Appendices
LEQUESNEL CAMP	16.3.17 (Cont.)		C section ordered to proceed to PUNCHY and establish Advanced Dressing Station, on arrival at MAUCOURT road three horsed CARTS found to be unsafe for transport, latter was left at Maucourt and personnel proceeded to PUNCHY. Remainder of 2nd A.C. proceeded to ROSIÈRES.	J.M.P.
		3 p.m.		arriving at 5 p.m.
ROSIÈRES	19.3.17		Proceeded to PUNCHY and thence to HYENCOURT LE PETIT for purpose of reconnoitering roads. Orders issued to O/C C section to collect transport from Maucourt and to proceed to HYENCOURT, on arrival to establish touch with R.M.O.s of 105th Inf. Brigade and form advanced dressing station, 12 hours with wheeled stretchers, to proceed to CHILLY and report to officer of 106 A.L. ½ wheeled stretcher party.	
"	20.3.17		Instructions received by wire from the Corps that sentence on Pte Dalton was approved; Suspension of former sentence removed and the two sentences to run concurrently.	J.M.P.
"	21.3.17		No. 45965 Pte Walter J. Paul committed to prison to undergo sentence awarded OTR by 29 C.C.S. and struck off strength.	

Army Form C. 2118

WAR DIARY
or
INTELLIGENCE SUMMARY

(Erase heading not required.)

105th FIELD AMBULANCE

Instructions regarding War Diaries and Intelligence Summaries are contained in F. S. Regs., Part II. and the Staff Manual respectively. Title Pages will be prepared in manuscript.

Place	Date	Hour	Summary of Events and Information	Remarks and references to Appendices
ROSIERES	22.3.17		All available men, working with two N.C.O's detailed for road repairing work N. of Fréchencourt to N. of Harancourt.	J.M.R
"	23.3.17		Road repairing continued. Party been withdrawn from advanced detachment to re-inforce working party.	J.M.R
"	24.3.17		Summers tent adopted from 11 p.m. Road repairing continued.	J.M.R
"	25.3.17		Nothing to report.	J.M.R
"	26.3.17		Road repairing continued. Party working towards Rosieres. Visited advanced detachment at Hyencourt le Petit. Lieut. R.S. Bull returned from leave and joined the unit. Acting on instructions from A.D.M.S. 35th Division, reconnoitred the villages of HARBONNIERES, MORCHAIN, PERTAIN, LICOURT, POTTE, and a room to hold an accommodation for 2 Lt. A. H. Lee and thirty patients.	J.M.R
"	28.3.17		Road repairing continued.	J.M.R

1875 Wt. W593/826 1,000,000 4/15 J.B.C.&A. A.D.S.S./Forms/C. 2118.

Army Form C. 2118

WAR DIARY
or
INTELLIGENCE SUMMARY
(Erase heading not required.)

105th FIELD AMBULANCE

Place	Date	Hour	Summary of Events and Information	Remarks and references to Appendices
ROSIERES	29.3.17	9.10 a.m.	Field Ambulance moved to OMIECOURT arriving at 2 p.m. Attached to and collected sick from 106th Inf Brigade. A section proceeded direct from HYENCOURT and joined main body at Omiecourt.	J.H.R.
OMIECOURT	30.3.17		Capt. J. M. MILLER detailed as officer i/c Divisional Hospital. Accommodation available in Sheds and Huts for thirty or forty sick. One horse Ambulance detailed to collect sick from 16th H.L.I. and 17th Royal Scots. One Horse Ambulance detailed to collect from 15th H.L.I. and 17th A.S.H. went Yoked. Map reference of Sta A.k. Bycester transport and A.S.C. personnel accommodated separately in village of OMIECOURT.	J.H.R.
"	31.3.17		Motor Ambulance detailed to collect sick from 18th Highland Light Infantry and 14th Royal Scots.	J.H.R.

J. H. Ryland
Lt. Col. R.A.M.C. 105 Field Ambulance

Confidential.

War Diary

of

105th Field Ambulance R.A.M.C.

From

1st April 1917

to

30th April 1917

Inclusive.

Volume XV   Original

Army Form C. 2118

WAR DIARY
or
INTELLIGENCE SUMMARY
105 FIELD AMBULANCE
(Erase heading not required.)

Place	Date	Hour	Summary of Events and Information	Remarks and references to Appendices
SOMIECOURT	1.4.17	11.30AM	105th Fd Amb. moved to MESNIL-ST NICAISE. Map reference 72 E 44 Divisions 3 copies in	JMR
MESNIL-ST NICAISE	2.4.17		Site prepared for occupation by Fd Amb. Accommodation for 40 to 50 patients provided in upper story of farm building.	JMR
"	3.4.17		Lt. Hill RAMC detailed to visit BOUY LE GRAND & LE PETIT daily to see French civilian sick.	JMR
"	4.4.17		Medical Board assembled to examine Lt. Broadhurst 19th L.N.L. Lt. G.S. Bull assumed charge of Labour Unit working nr Chaulnes i/c J.E. 120 Fd. Coy R.E. Railway Const. opened to O.C. Capt. Grant detailed to see sick of 4th Lab Coy. Northants Regt. at MARCHELEPOT daily.	JMR
"	5.4.17		Unit visited by A.D.M.S. 35th Division.	JMR
"	6.4.17		Nothing to report.	JMR
"	7.4.17		Capt. S. I. M. Offr. Rawl proceeded to assume medical charge of following units at last due at Herbecourt:- 4 Co 10 Light Rly Coy, No 8 Regimental Rly and attached details, No 2 Sect. 330 Roads Constl Coy.	JMR

Army Form C. 2118

WAR DIARY or INTELLIGENCE SUMMARY

(Erase heading not required.) **105 FIELD AMBULANCE**

Place	Date	Hour	Summary of Events and Information	Remarks and references to Appendices
MESNIL-ST NICAISE	7/4/17		(Cont:) 1 N.C.O. and 2 men temporarily attached 107th Fd. Amb. for duty.	JHR
"	8/4/17		B Section less motor ambulances and with 2 horse Ambulances proceeded to Capt. R.H. Muller R.A.M.C. to MOLIGNAUX to form advanced collecting posts. O.C. attached from Battalion of 106 Inf. Bde and forwarded to Fd. Ops. 105 Fd. Amb. Lieut. A.S. Bell R.A.M.C. detailed to take over duties of Capt. Grant on latter proceeding to Molignaux. 1 M.O. and 10 men proceeded to No. 36 C.C.S. for temporary duty.	JHR
"	9/4/17		15 men attached 107th Fd. Amb. for temporary duty.	JHR
"	10/4/17 11.30 p.m.		Remainder of Fd. Amb. proceeded to MOLIGNAUX and formed advanced section, arriving 3.30 p.m. All detachments returned from 107th Fd. Amb.	JHR
"	11/4/17 9 A.M.		105th Fd. Amb. proceeded to TERTRY arriving 11.0 A.M. and took over from a Fd. Amb. of 61st Division. Three Hospital Marquees taken over	JHR

Army Form C. 2118

WAR DIARY
or
INTELLIGENCE SUMMARY

(Erase heading not required.) 105th FIELD AMBULANCE.

Place	Date	Hour	Summary of Events and Information	Remarks and references to Appendices
TERTRY	11.4.17		Capt. Grant, Lieut. Hill and 54 O.R. proceeded to Vermand to form advanced dressing station. Capt. Muller and 14 O.R. proceeded to POEUILLY to form bearer advanced dressing station. Cases from aid post in VADENCOURT went to Crater in front of BIHECOURT by stretcher, thence by aid car to VERMAND. Relay post established in Bihecourt. Horse Ambulances utilised to collect sick daily from CAULAINCOURT, MERAUCOURT and MONCHY-LAGACHE. Capt. McAfee returned from HARBONNIERES.	App.
"	12.4.17		1 W.O. and 10 men returned from to 36. C.C.S.	App.
"	13.4.17		No. 63987 Pte Amsent W.J. proceeded to ABBEVILLE for transfer to Rly Signal Service Ref under authority 35th Div. 5926/9 of 11.4.17	App
"	14.4.17		2 N.C.Os. 9.24 men attached 106th W.N. Amb. for temporary duty as reinforcement of Stretcher Bearers.	App

WAR DIARY or INTELLIGENCE SUMMARY

Army Form C. 2118

105th FIELD AMBULANCE

Place	Date	Hour	Summary of Events and Information	Remarks and references to Appendices
JERTRY	15/4/17		Horse Ambulance attached for duty with 106th Lt.M.A.T. struck by a shell while proceeding up the MAISSEMY Road, the undermentioned men and both horses were killed — T/042308 L/Cp FANNING.T C.S.C.(H.T.) attached 105th L.M.A.T and No 63781 Pte ABRAM.J Rm C 105th Fd A.A.	G.H.R.
"	16/4/17		Am Ambulance wagon damaged by shell fire taken to ordnance and condemned by them as unfit for repair. New wagon ordered for.	G.H.R.
"	17/4/17		105th Fd A.A. joined Advanced party at VERMAND arriving at 1.0 pm. Eight hospital marquees including four received on 14.4.17, struck at JERBY and conveyed to VERMAND. Camp pitched in field adjoining the Tournelles, 2 marquees being used for mess Receiving Rooms and 2 Wards each composed of 3 marquees together.	G.H.R.
VERMAND	18/4/17		Nothing to report.	G.H.R.
"	19/4/17		Visit by G.O.C. 35th Division.	G.H.R.

WAR DIARY
or
INTELLIGENCE SUMMARY

(Erase heading not required.)

Army Form C. 2118

105th FIELD AMBULANCE.

Place	Date	Hour	Summary of Events and Information	Remarks and references to Appendices
VERMAND	20.4.17		Lieut. R.S. Bull proceeded for duty with 17 Lane. Fusiliers vice Capt. Bryant Evacuated Sick.	J.H.R.
"	21.4.17		Straining of Hospital marquees continued. Shelters erected for cookhouse, A.D's stores, Pack Store, and for horses personnel.	J.H.R.
"	22.4.17		Work on Baths at Bihecourt finished pending Class to evacuate direct from A.D. Post. Relay post at Bihecourt dispensed with and party together with Supplies, blankets and stretchers stationed at A.D.post. Motors to report.	J.H.R.
"	23.4.17 24.4.17		Capt helped on 18 men proceeded to Château Grounds at R.1.0.95 to establish Advanced Dressing Station.	J.H.R.
"	25.4.17		Shelter built of logs and sand bags erected at A.D.S. providing accommodation for dressing wounded and for 6 stretchers. Lieut S.D. Adam R.A.M.C. proceeded to England on expiry of contract G.O. is shock. Lieut Tyson granted leave from 25.4.17 to 5.5.17	J.H.R.
"				J.H.R.

WAR DIARY
or
INTELLIGENCE SUMMARY

Army Form C. 2118

105th FIELD AMBULANCE

Place	Date	Hour	Summary of Events and Information	Remarks and references to Appendices
VERMAND	26.4.17		Nothing to report.	J.H.R.
"	27.4.17		Four steel cupolas obtained from 2nd & 3rd by R.E and erected at A.D.S forming a shelter capable of accommodating 12 sitting cases.	J.H.R.
"	28.4.17	11.30 p.m	Orders received from A.D.M.S. 3rd Div. to reinforce the A.D.S. with 1 officer, 18 O.R. and 2 lm tram cars. Completion ordered at 2 a.m. Capt. Miller RAMC proceeded as officer i/c party.	J.H.R.
"	29.4.17		The O.C. was proceeded to the A.D.S for the purpose of conveying to this thence to the R.A.P 12 men also proceeded to the R.A.P to erect a shelter and prepare a track for stretcher Notchers.	J.H.R.
"	30.1.17		Nothing to report.	J.H.R.

J H Richard
Lieut. Col. RAMC
O C 105 F. A.

Confidential

140/2161

War Diary

of

105th Field Ambulance R.A.M.C.

From

1st May 1917

to

31st May 1917.

Inclusive.

Volume XVI.

Original.

COMMITTEE FOR THE MEDICAL HISTORY OF THE WAR
Date 10 JUL 1917

WAR DIARY
INTELLIGENCE SUMMARY
105th FIELD AMBULANCE

Army Form C. 2118

Place	Date	Hour	Summary of Events and Information	Remarks and references to Appendices
VERMAND	1.5.17		Site occupied by 106th Fd. Amb. Subjected to hostile shelling. All cases (42 in num-ber) transferred to this unit. Work at A.D.S. in VADENCOURT Chateau Grounds completed (Map reference Sheet 62.C. R16.B.) One large dressing room built in an old German gun pit; upright posts and roof made of pine logs from cut down trees; front wall consists of iron gates and two layers of sand bags; over logs on roof one two layers of sand bags, one layer of corrugated iron, a layer of earth six inches thick & finally branches of trees acting as camouflage. Accommodation available for dressing two cases at once, a rack to hold three stretchers & floor space sufficient for four stretchers. Adjacent to dressing room a trench has been widened (sufficient to take a stretcher), deepened and a roof still in edge of trench and covered with a layer of sand bags (6 sand bags thick) made covering sections of old German cupolas, placed side by side. Accommodation of latter sufficient for twelve stretchers or twenty sitting cases. All material used available locally except sand bags.	J.H.R.
"	2.5.17		Lieut. R.J. HELSBY. R.A.M.C. posted to 105th Fd. An. b. as re-inforcement.	J.H.R.
"	3.5.17		Nothing to report.	J.H.R.
"	4.5.17		Nothing to report.	J.H.R.

WAR DIARY
or
INTELLIGENCE SUMMARY
(Erase heading not required.)

105 FIELD AMBULANCE

Army Form C. 2118

Place	Date	Hour	Summary of Events and Information	Remarks and references to Appendices
VERMAND	5.5.17	11 A.M.	Medical Board assembled to examine W/m. officers for commissions in R.F.C. 2/Lt. PLANT. 2/Lt. LEWIS. 2/Lt. JOHNSON. all of 15th Sherwood Foresters. Lieut. BULL proceeded to 14th Lancs Fusiliers for duty & struck off strength.	App.
"	6.5.17		Lieut. HILL proceeded to 13th Cheshires for Temporary duty in relief of Capt. BRIGGS R.A.M.C. Latter officer proceeded to 105th Fd. A.R. for Temporary duty for 14 days. Capt. Briggs alloted No O/c A ward. Lieut. Kelsby alloted No O/c B ward. No 54888 Corpl. Northwood G evacuated sick to No 21 CCS & struck off strength. Lieut. A.B. MacCARTHY RAMC posted to 105th Fd. A.R. as re-inforcement & taken on strength.	App.
"	7.5.17		Nothing to report.	
"	8.5.17		Shelter, under sec of tumulus, for accommodation of patients in the event of the Camp being shelled, completed.	App.
"	9.5.17		Capt. J.M. MILLER RAMC proceeded on leave to England from 9.5.17 to 19.5.17	App.

Army Form C. 2118

WAR DIARY
or
INTELLIGENCE SUMMARY
(Erase heading not required.)

105th FIELD AMBULANCE.

Instructions regarding War Diaries and Intelligence Summaries are contained in F. S. Regs., Part II. and the Staff Manual respectively. Title Pages will be prepared in manuscript.

Place	Date	Hour	Summary of Events and Information	Remarks and references to Appendices
VERMAND	10.5.17		Lieut. MacCarthy posted as O/c Tent Subdivision A Section.	
			" " " " B "	
			No. 74/041295 Cpl. Williams. T. A.S.C. (H.T.) evacuated sick to No. 21 C.C.S. and struck off strength.	S.R.
"	11.5.17		Capt. J.M. Grant. R.A.M.C. proceeded for duty with 19th D.L.I. in relief of Capt. Barrs.	S.R.
"	12.5.17		Nothing to report.	S.R.
"	13.5.17		Nothing to report.	S.R.
"	14.5.17		Board of Survey assembled to examine Winter Clothing. President. Lieut Richard R.A.M.C. Members. Capt. Hegarty. Lieut J. The Tyson R.A.M.C. Capt. The After Lt. MacCarthy and party at A.D.S. reported train today. No.63667 Pte Norman. H. evacuated sick to No. 21 C.C.S. and struck off strength. No. 54888 Cpl Northward discharged from No. 21 C.C.S. & rejoined on strength	S.R.

WAR DIARY
of
INTELLIGENCE SUMMARY
(Erase heading not required.)

105th FIELD AMBULANCE.

Army Form C. 2118

Place	Date	Hour	Summary of Events and Information	Remarks and references to Appendices
VERMAND	15.5.17.		RamC No 63914 Pte Kieran W. Evacuated sick to No 21 C.C.S. & Struck off Strength.	JpR
"	16.5.17		No 770928 & 22 Dr Barnard B.J. RSC (AT) Evacuated sick to No 21 C.C.S and Struck off Strength. No 63498 Pte Hamilton J. RAMC Evacuated sick to No 21 CCS & Struck off Strength.	JpR
"	17.5.17.		Capt. Briggs RamC returned to 15th Cheshires relieving Lt Neil RamC. Latter rejoined 105th Fd A.A. Lieut Hill, 3 NCOs and 3 men proceeded as advance party to XV Corps Main Dressing Station.	JpR
"	18.5.17.		No 69889 Pte Pinkstone A.C. RamC Evacuated sick to No 21 C.C.S & Struck off Strength.	JpR
"	19.5.17. 6.30am		All hospital marquees struck and, together with large numbers of shelters and blankets despatched to No 21 C.C.S. 105 Fd Amb. left Vermand. Marched with 106th Inf. Brigade and arrived at PERONNE at 11 AM.	JpR JpR

Army Form C. 2118

WAR DIARY
or
INTELLIGENCE SUMMARY
(Erase heading not required.)

105th FIELD AMBULANCE

Place	Date	Hour	Summary of Events and Information	Remarks and references to Appendices
PERONNE	20/5/17	8.30 p.m.	105th Fd. Amb. left PERONNE. Marched to ½ S. of FINS. (Map ref. sheet 57C V18c08) Arriving 11.45 P.M. Took over XV Corps main Dressing Station from 26th Fd. Amb. All motor ambulances, with exception of one Sunbeam and all wheeled stretcher carriers detailed for duty with 106th Fd. Amb.	JWR
FINS	21/5/17		XV Corps Main Dressing Station is situated in a field on gently sloping ground, half a mile S. of FINS. A semi-circular made road, 300 yards long, leads off and on to the FINS—NURLU road, and gives access to Cars. Thirty small IP marquees and several Nissen huts provide accommodation for walk-in cases and a spray bath installed. Electric light is provided by a dynamo worked by a small I.C. petrol Engine. Operating theatre is a large Nissen hut. Overhead lighting is provided by Windows running along the entire length of the roof. All sick are shown as transfers and all wounded as direct admissions from Fd. Ambulances. Evacuation to C.C.S. at PERONNE is carried out by No 20 M.A.C.	JWR

1875 Wt. W593/826 1,000,000 4/15 J.B.C. & A. A.D.S.S./Forms/C.2118.

Army Form C. 2118

WAR DIARY
or
INTELLIGENCE SUMMARY

(Erase heading not required.)

105 FIELD AMBULANCE

Place	Date	Hour	Summary of Events and Information	Remarks and references to Appendices
FINS	22/5/17		One clerk returned to 60th Fd. Amb.	
"	23/5/17		Capt. Stewart RAMC and Tent Subdivision of 2nd Fd. Amb. rejoined their unit and are struck off strength of Capt. M.D. Station.	
"	24/5/17		Capt. Ford RAMC and 2 O.R's / East Lancs. 2/6 Bn L. arrived for duty at C.M.D.S.	
"	25/5/17		Nothing to report.	
"	26/5/17		Capt. A McBrother RAMC evacuated sick to No 34 C.C.S. Proven. Capt. Ford RAMC detailed as h.O/c 6 Division.	
"	27/5/17		Lieut. MacCarthy RAMC detailed as h.O/c C Division in relief of Capt. Ford, latter officer detailed to assume charge of B Division	
"	28/5/17		Nothing to report.	

Army Form C. 2118

WAR DIARY
or
INTELLIGENCE SUMMARY
(Erase heading not required.) 105th FIELD AMBULANCE

Place	Date	Hour	Summary of Events and Information	Remarks and references to Appendices
FINS	29/5/17		No 638-54 Sgt. CART. W Ram C detailed to attend course of instruction in gas at 20th Divisional School.	J.R.
"	30/5/17		Pte Tod and Bmd. Ram C proceed on leave from 31.5.17 to 9.6.17.	J.R.
"	31/5/17		Nothing to report.	

J.R. Rickart
Lieut Col Ram C
O.C. 105th Field Ambulance.

APPENDIX.

XVth Corps Main Dressing Station. Summaries of Sick States.

From 20/5/17 to 21/5/17

Division	Remaining		Admitted		To Main bas		To Corps Rest Sta		To Corps Sick Sta		Duty		Died		Remaining	
	O	O.R	O	O.R	O	O.R	O	O.R	O	O.R	O	O.R	O	O.R	Officers	Other Ranks
8th	1	74		16		10		5		1		2			1	72
20th	2	173		40		13		4		1		8			2	187
35th		4								1						3
40th	3	198		22		13		12				1			3	194
Other Formations		77	1	53	1	6						3				121
	6	526	1	131	1	42		21		3		14			6	577

From 21/5/17 to 22/5/17

Division	Remaining		Admitted		To C.C.S.		To C.R.S.		To C.S.S.		Duty		Died		Remaining	
	O	O.R	O	O.R	O	O.R	O	O.R	O	O.R	O	O.R	O	O.R	Officers	Other Ranks
8th	1	72	4	20	3	15	1	2		2		2			1	71
20th	2	187	1	48		32						8			3	195
35th		3								3						
40th	3	194	3	63	1	53	2			3		7			3	194
42nd		71		49		18		2		5						95
Other Formations		50		22		14				1		1				56
	6	577	8	202	4	132	3	4		14		18			7	611

From 22/5/17 to 23/5/17

Division	Remaining		Admitted		To C.C.S.		To C.R.S.		To C.S.S.		Duty		Died		Remaining	
	O	O.R	O	O.R	O	O.R	O	O.R	O	O.R	O	O.R	O	O.R	Officers	Other Ranks
8th	1	71		22		11		5				2			1	75
20th	3	195	1	19	1	23	2	17		3		2			1	169
35th			1	16	1	2				3						11
40th	3	194		25	1	21		24		3		12			2	159
42nd		95		49		14	2			18		1				109
Other Formations		56		29		10	1			2		4				68
	7	611	2	160	3	81	2	49		29		21			4	591

XVth Corps Main Dressing Station. Summaries of Sick States.

From 23/5/17 to 24/5/17

Division	Remaining	Admitted	To C.C.S	To C.R.S	C.S.S	Duty	Died	Remaining
	O / O.R	O / O.R	O / O.R	O / O.R	O / O.R	O / O.R	O / O.R	O / O.R
8th	1 / 75	2 / 17	3	1 / 12		3		2 / 74
20th	1 / 169	1 / 25	5	2 / 27	1	7		154
35th	11	1 / 31	5		4		1	33
40th	2 / 159	2 / 16	17	24	1	5		4 / 128
42nd	109	30	10	14	10	1		104
Other Formation	68	31	5	3		2		89
	4 / 591	6 / 150	45	3 / 80	16	18	1	6 / 582

From 24/5/17 to 25/5/17

Division	Remaining	Admtd	To C.C.S	To C.R.S	C.S.S	Duty	Died	Remaining Officers	Other Ranks
	O / O.R	O / O.R	O / O.R	O / O.R	O / O.R	O / O.R	O / O.R		
8th	2 / 74	10	4	8		2		2	70
20th	154		2	12		4			136
35th	33	2 / 43	9	3	11			2	53
40th	4 / 128	1 / 14	1 / 4	9	1	6		4	122
42nd	104	43	10	7	5	4			121
59th									
Other Formation	89	25	8	10	2	2			92
	6 / 582	3 / 135	1 / 37	49	19	18		8	594

From 25/5/17 to 26/5/17

Division	Remaining	Admtd	To C.C.S	To C.R.S	C.S.S	Duty	Died	Remaining Officers	Other Ranks
	O / O.R	O / O.R	O / O.R	O / O.R	O / O.R	O / O.R	O / O.R		
8th	2 / 70	1 / 13	2 / 4	1 / 4		3			72
20th	136	2	4	10		3			121
35th	2 / 53	4 / 12	2 / 5	5	1			4	54
40th	4 / 122	3 / 43	3 / 16	1 / 9	1	12	1	3	126
42nd	121	2 / 50	19	10	6	2		2	134
59th		1 / 3	1 / 2						1
Other Formation	92	16	17	4	2	1			84
	8 / 594	11 / 139	8 / 67	2 / 42	10	21	1	9	592

XV th Corps Main Dressing Station. Summaries of Sick States.

From 26/5/17 to 27/5/17.

Division	Remaining		Admitted		To C.C.S		To C.R.S		To C.S.S		Duty		Died		Remaining	
	O	O.R	O	O.R	O	O.R	O	O.R	O	O.R	O	O.R	O	O.R	Officers	Other Ranks
8th		72		24		12						1				83
20th		121		1		3		1		1		10				107
35th	4	54	4	33	5	5						2			3	80
40th	3	126	1	21		24	1				4	4			3	115
42nd	2	134		65		20					9	4	1		2	165
59th		1		1		1										1
Other Formation		84	3	35	3	17					1	3				98
	9	592	8	180	8	82	1	1			15	24	1		8	649

From 27/5/17 to 28/5/17.

Division	Remaining		Admitted		To C.C.S		To C.R.S		To C.S.S		Duty		Died		Remaining	
	O	O.R	O	O.R	O	O.R	O	O.R	O	O.R	O	O.R	O	O.R	Officers	Other Ranks
8th		83	1	34	1	10		4				3				100
20th		107				1		9				15				82
35th	3	80	2	23	2	9		4	1	1		1			2	88
40th	3	115	1	26		16	2	10				13			2	102
42nd	2	165	1	57	1	19		9	5			9			2	180
59th		1		2		10	1			1						11
Other Formation		98		17		8		4				5				98
	8	649	7	167	5	63	3	40	6	1		46			6	661

From 28/5/17 to 29/5/17.

Division	Remaining		Admitted		To C.C.S		To C.R.S		To C.S.S		Duty		Died		Remaining	
	O	O.R	O	O.R	O	O.R	O	O.R	O	O.R	O	O.R	O	O.R	Officers	Other Ranks
8th		100	3	43	3	6		6				1				130
20th		82				3		6				7				66
35th	2	88	4	21	1	15		2		1		2			5	89
40th	2	102	1	4	2	6		5		1		6			1	88
42nd	2	180	3	59	3	8	1	7	18			8			1	198
59th		11	1	3		2									1	12
Other Formation		98	1	20	1	8		5	2			6				97
	6	661	13	150	10	48	1	31	22			30			8	680

XV Corps Main Dressing Station. Summaries of Sick States.

From 29/5/17 to 30/5/17

Division	Remaining		Admitted		to C.C.S		to C.R.S		to C.S.S		Duty		Died		Remaining Officers	Other Ranks
	O	O.R	O	O.R	O	O.R	O	O.R	O	O.R	O	O.R	O	O.R		
8th		130		22		4		7		1						140
20th		66						5				7				54
35th	5	89	1	32		12	2	4	1			10			3	95
40th	1	88	1	10	1	8	1	5				13				72
42nd	1	148	2	24	1	10		3		4		14			2	191
59th	1	12	1	2		1									2	13
Other Formation		97		19		13		4				4				95
	8	680	5	109	2	48	3	28	1	5		48			7	660

From 30/5/17 to 31/5/17

Division	Remaining		Admitted		to C.C.S		to C.R.S		to C.S.S		Duty		Died		Remaining Officers	Other Ranks
	O	O.R	O	O.R	O	O.R	O	O.R	O	O.R	O	O.R	O	O.R		
8th		140	3	27	2	8		8							1	151
20th		54						7				12				35
35th	3	95	1	27	1	6		3				13			3	100
40th		72	1	13	1	11		4				11				59
42nd	2	191	1	30		12		13				20			3	176
59th	2	13		18		8		1				1			2	21
Other Formation		95		22		8		4				10				95
	7	660	6	137	4	53		40				67			9	637

Confidential.

War Diary

of

105th Field Ambulance. R.A.M.C.

From

1st June 1917.

to

30th June 1917.

Inclusive.

Volume XVII   Original.

WAR DIARY OR INTELLIGENCE SUMMARY

Army Form C. 2118

105th FIELD AMBULANCE

Place	Date	Hour	Summary of Events and Information	Remarks and references to Appendices
FINS.	1/6/17		Capt. E. Phillips, R.A.M.C. (Regular) late D.A.D.M.S. 8th Division posted to 105th Fd Amb. and taken on strength from 1/6/17. To join on completion of ten days leave.	JHR
"	2/6/17		XV Corps relieved by III Corps. Main Dressing Station taken over by latter. No. T/28682 D. MKell. T.H. A.S.C. (H.T.) transferred to no 2 Corp Div. Train and struck off strength of unit. No. 14/064 343 Dr Bergan J. F. transferred from no 2 Corp. Div. Train and taken on strength.	JHR
"	3/6/17		1 N.C.O and 10 men from 2/2 N. Midland Fd. Amb. attached to C.M.D.S. for Constitutional work. Also 1 N.C.O and 10 men from 137 Fd. Amb.	JHR
"	4/6/17		One Sergeant clerk from 2/3 North Midland Fd. A.R. attached to C.M.D.S.	JHR
"	5/6/17		Nothing to report.	JHR
"	6/6/17		2 N.C.Os and 28 men from 1/3 E. Lancs. Fd. A.b. returned to their unit.	JHR
"	7/6/17		Nothing to report.	JHR

Army Form C. 2118

WAR DIARY
or
INTELLIGENCE SUMMARY

(Erase heading not required.)

105 & 2 FIELD AMBULANCE

Instructions regarding War Diaries and Intelligence Summaries are contained in F.S. Regs., Part II. and the Staff Manual respectively. Title Pages will be prepared in manuscript.

Place	Date	Hour	Summary of Events and Information	Remarks and references to Appendices
FINS.	8/6/17		10 O.R. from 2/1 N. Midland Fd. A.L. attached to C.M.D.S. for Construction work.	JHR.
"	9/6/17		Nothing to report.	JHR.
"	10/6/17		90546 Sgt. Offer R.J. and 90699 Pte Padgett J.J. proceeded to duty at III Corps Convalescent Depôt.	JHR.
"	11/6/17		Nothing to report.	JHR.
"	12/6/17		Re-organization of C.M.D.S. proceeding. Accommodation for gas cases provided in old Indian pattern H.P. marquees re-pitched in four rows. Each row being formed of 5 tents joined together to make one ward. Accommodation for sitting cases provided in new H.P. marquees; pitched in one block of six rows, each now composed of 4 tents forming one ward. Separate accommodation is being provided for treatment of gas cases, six new Indian pattern marquees being pitched and joined to form one ward, with an annexe of 2 tents for officers.	JHR.
"	13/6/17		Nothing to report.	JHR.

WAR DIARY
or
INTELLIGENCE SUMMARY

(Erase heading not required.)   105th FIELD AMBULANCE.

Army Form C. 2118

Place	Date	Hour	Summary of Events and Information	Remarks and references to Appendices
FINS	14/6/17		Two Adrian huts delivered at C.M.D.S. by order of D.D.M.S. III Corps Proposed to be used, one as a Dining Room sited close to the Cook house; the other as a Dressing Room for wounded & Dispensary.	JHR
"	15/6/17		Farrier Robson. H. and Dr. Gleaves P.g. A.S.C.(H.T) posted to 105 Fd.A.E 9 taken on strength. P.te J. Sow. A. Ram.C posted to 105 Fd.A.K. 9 taken on strength	JHR
"	16/6/17		Weekly Inspection of Horse Transport by A.A.D.V.S 85 Division. Capt. E. Phillps returned from leave.	JHR
"	17/6/17		Capt. E. Phillps proceeded for duty at office of D.D.M.S III Corps.	JHR
"	18/6/17		Demonstration on use of Horse Respirators by N.C.O detailed by Div.^l Gas Officer. Capt. C.W. Fort. Ram.C returned to 1/1 East Lancs. Fd. Am. C.	JHR

WAR DIARY or INTELLIGENCE SUMMARY

Army Form C. 2118

105th FIELD AMBULANCE.

Place	Date	Hour	Summary of Events and Information	Remarks and references to Appendices
FINS	19/6/17		T4/041556 B⁄S Farrier Sergt. W. ASC (H.T.) appointed A/Farrier Corpl. with pay from 11/5/17. (Authority A.G. Base P12/4889 dated 13.6.17).	JMR
"	20/6/17		Nothing to report.	JMR
"	21/6/17		Nothing to report.	JMR
"	22/6/17		M2/031647 A/Sgt. Wilson A.E. ASC (M.T.) promoted Sergeant from 14.6.17. M2/036040 A/Cpl. Hopkins W. ASC (M.T.) promoted Corporal from 14.6.17. A.S.C. Records Authority P11/4469.	JMR
"	23/6/17		Lt. C. R. Hall. RAMC proceeded on leave from 23.6.17 to 3.7.17. Followin N.C.O.s and men sent posted to 105th Fd. Amb. and taken on strength. 365265 Pte Bevan. P.G. 368055 Pte Jones. W.N. 364176 Pte Morgan N.B. 366415 Pte Owens R.J. 364408 Pte Pickens. D.	JMR
"	24/6/17		That subdivision of 1/3 E. Lancs Fd. A.b. less two clerks returned to its unit.	JMR

WAR DIARY
or
INTELLIGENCE SUMMARY
(Erase heading not required.)

Army Form C. 2118

105th FIELD AMBULANCE.

Place	Date	Hour	Summary of Events and Information	Remarks and references to Appendices
FINS.	25/6/17		Tent sub-div. of 2/2 W. Midland Fd. A.L. attacked on 8th inst. returned to their unit.	JMR
"	26/6/17		69885 Pte Pinkstone R.C. posted to 105th Fd. A.L. and taken on strength.	JMR
"	27/6/17		Nothing to report.	JMR
"	28/6/17		Alteration in evacuation of cases to C.R.S. Cases now leave M.D.S. Sirius at 8 A.M. Arrive at Guinness at 9:15 P.M. and proceed at 10 P.M. by supply train on road gauge.	JMR
"	29/6/17		Nothing to report.	JMR
"	30/6/17		Capt. J.M. Miller R.A.M.C. evacuated sick to 34 C.C.S. on 26/75 struck off strength.	JMR

J.M. Rickards
Lieut. R.A.M.C.
O.C. 105th Field Ambulance.

APPENDIX

XVth Corps Main Dressing Station. Daily Sick States.

From 31/5/17 to 1/6/17

DIVISION	REMAINING	ADMITTED	TO C.C.S	TO C.R.S	TO C.S.S	DUTY	DIED	REMAINING
	O / O.R	O / O.R	O / O.R	O / O.R	O / O.R	O / O.R	O / O.R	Officers / Other Ranks
8th	1 / 151	/ 6	/ 6	/ 11		/ 7		1 / 133
20th	/ 35			/ 2		/ 8		/ 25
35th	3 / 100	1 / 23	1 / 6	2 / 3	/ 1	/ 3		1 / 110
40th	/ 59	1 / 6	1 / 4	/ 2		/ 3		/ 56
42nd	3 / 176	4 / 23	2 / 16	/ 7	/ 1	/ 11		5 / 164
59th	2 / 21	1 / 21	1 / 10	/ 2				2 / 29
Other Formations	/ 95	2 / 21	1 / 11	/ 2		/ 11		1 / 92
Prisoners		/ 1	/ 1					
	9 / 637	9 / 101	6 / 54	2 / 29	/ 3	/ 43		10 / 609

IIIrd Corps Main Dressing Station

From 1/6/17 to 2/6/17

DIVISION	REMAINING	ADMITTED	TO C.C.S	TO C.R.S	TO C.S.S	DUTY	DIED	REMAINING
	O / O.R	O / O.R	O / O.R	O / O.R	O / O.R	O / O.R	O / O.R	O / O.R
8th	1 / 133		1 / 1	/ 1		/ 26		/ 105
20th	/ 25					/ 4		/ 21
35th	1 / 110	2 / 23	1 / 4		/ 1	/ 13		2 / 115
40th	/ 56	3 / 24	3 / 6			/ 7		/ 67
42nd	5 / 164	1 / 30	1 / 20	/ 1	/ 2	/ 23	1 /	3 / 149
59th	2 / 29	2 / 14	2 / 4			/ 2	/ 2	2 / 35
Other Formations	1 / 92	/ 28	1 / 14			/ 19		/ 87
	10 / 609	8 / 119	9 / 49	1 / 1	/ 3	/ 94	1 / 2	7 / 579

From 2/6/17 to 3/6/17

DIVISION	REMAINING	ADMITTED	TO C.C.S	TO C.R.S	TO C.S.S	DUTY	DIED	REMAINING
	O / O.R	O / O.R	O / O.R	O / O.R	O / O.R	O / O.R	O / O.R	O / O.R
8th	/ 105		/ 1	/ 13		/ 9		/ 82
20th	/ 21			/ 2		/ 1		/ 18
35th	2 / 115	1 / 52	/ 21	/ 6		/ 5	/ 3	3 / 135
40th	/ 67	1 / 42	1 / 13	/ 5		/ 5		/ 86
42nd	3 / 149	1 / 66	1 / 37	/ 12		/ 11	4 / 3	3 / 150
59th	2 / 35	4 / 27	4 / 7	/ 1	/ 1	/ 3	/ 2	2 / 50
Other Formations	/ 87	/ 23	/ 13	/ 10		/ 4		/ 83
French		/ 1	/ 1					
	7 / 579	7 / 210	6 / 93	/ 49	/ 1	/ 38	4 / 8	8 / 604

IIIrd Corps Main Dressing Station Daily Sick States.

From 3/6/17 to 4/6/17.

Division	Remaining		Admitted		To C.C.S.		To C.R.S.		To Corps Sta.		Scabies		Duty		Died		Remaining.	
	O	O.R.	O	O.R.	O	O.R.	O	O.R.	O	O.R.	O	O.R.	O	O.R.	O	O.R.	O	O.R.
8th		82				3								3				76
20th		18																18
35th	3	135	2	33	2	8								8			3	152
40th		86	3	19	3	13								3				89
42nd	3	150	4	71	5	30								10		1	2	180
59th	2	50		17		3								1			2	63
Other Formations		83	2	20	2	8								10				85
	8	604	11	160	12	65								35		1	7	663

From 4/6/17 to 5/6/17.

Division	Remaining		Admitted		To C.C.S.		To C.R.S.		To Corps Sta.		Scabies		Duty		Died		Remaining	
	O	O.R.	O	O.R.	O	O.R.	O	O.R.	O	O.R.	O	O.R.	O	O.R.	O	O.R.	O	O.R.
8th		76				1		6						12				57
20th		18						1						2				15
35th	3	152	2	24	2	6		10						7		1	3	152
40th		89	4	16	4	4		4		5								92
42nd	2	180		48		8	2	16		5				12				187
59th	2	63		11		3	1	4						3			1	64
Other Formations		85	1	27	1	12		5		2				4				89
	7	663	7	126	7	34	3	46		12				40		1	4	656

From 5/6/17 to 6/6/17.

Division	Remaining		Admitted		To C.C.S.		To C.R.S.		To Corps Sta.		Scabies		Duty		Died		Remaining.	
	O	O.R.	O	O.R.	O	O.R.	O	O.R.	O	O.R.	O	O.R.	O	O.R.	O	O.R.	O	O.R.
8th		57				1		6						8				42
20th		15						1										14
35th	3	152	2	33	1	5		11						6			4	163
40th		92		17		9		2		2				6				90
42nd		187	1	30	1	12		7				4		14				180
59th	1	64	2	19	1	6		1						4			2	72
Other Formations		89	1	19	1	6		3		1				10				88
	4	656	6	118	4	39		31		7				48			6	649

III Corps Main Dressing Station. Daily Sick States.

From 6/6/17 to 7/6/17

Division	Remaining		Admitted		To CCS		To CRS		To CSS		Duty		Died		Remaining	
	O	O.R	O	O.R	O	O.R	O	O.R	O	O.R	O	O.R	O	O.R	O	O.R
8th		42				1		4				3				34
20th		14						4								10
35th	4	163	2	22	1	8	2	16			1	11			2	150
40th		90	1	23	1	13		6	1			9				84
42nd		180		37		8		19		4		15		1		170
59th	2	72	2	13		6	2	3				5			2	71
Other Formations		88	1	26		9	1	10				7				88
	6	649	6	121	2	45	5	58		5	1	54		1	4	607

From 7/6/17 to 8/6/17

Division	Remaining		Admitted		To C.C.S		To C.R.S		To C.S.S		Duty		Died		Remaining	
	O	O.R	O	O.R	O	O.R	O	O.R	O	O.R	O	O.R	O	O.R	O	O.R
8th		34				1		2				3				28
20th		10				1						1				8
35th	2	150	1	34	3	4		12				20				148
40th		84	1	12	1	5		10		1		6				74
42nd		170	5	41	4	9		15				13			1	174
59th	2	71	2	38	4	10		5		1		2				91
Other Formations		88	1	27	1	10		10		1		9				85
	4	607	10	152	13	39		55		3		54			1	608

From 8/6/17 to 9/6/17

Division	Remaining		Admitted		To C.C.S		To C.R.S		To C.S.S		Duty		Died		Remaining	
	O	O.R	O	O.R	O	O.R	O	O.R	O	O.R	O	O.R	O	O.R	O	O.R
8th		28				1		1				3				23
20th		8				1		2								5
35th		148	2	26	2	12		14		2		8				138
40th		74		17		14		9		2		5				61
42nd	1	174	1	59	2	19		10		2		8				194
59th		91		25		7		6				2				101
Other Formations		85	1	15	1	4		7		1		6				82
	1	608	4	142	5	58		49		7		32				604

III Corps Main Dressing Station. Daily Sick States.

From 9/6/17 to 10/6/17

DIVISION	REMAINING		ADMITTED		TO CAS CLG STA		TO CORPS REST STA		TO CORPS SCABIES STA		DUTY		DIED		REMAINING	
	O	O.R	O	O.R	O	O.R	O	O.R	O	O.R	O	O.R	O	O.R	O	O.R
8th		23				1						2				20
20th		5														5
35th		138	2	39	2	9				2		8				158
40th		61	1	16	1	12						6				59
42nd		194		56		21				1		11		2		215
59th		101	1	20	1	5						3				113
Ochu.Formation		82		23		9				1		6				89
				1		1										
		604	4	155	4	58				4		36		2		659

From 10/6/17 to 11/6/17

DIVISION	REMAINING		ADMITTED		TO C.C.S.		TO C.R.S.		TO C.S.S.		DUTY		DIED		REMAINING	
	O	O.R	O	O.R	O	O.R	O	O.R	O	O.R	O	O.R	O	O.R	O	O.R
8th		20				1		1								18
20th		5				1										4
35th		158		58		10		7				2				197
40th		59	1	3	1	8		2								52
42nd		215	1	46	1	23		8		2				1		227
59th		113	1	34		13		3				1			1	130
Ochu.Formation		89	1	20	1	2		4				1				102
		659	4	161	3	58		25		2		4		1	1	730

From 11/6/17 to 12/6/17

DIVISION	REMAINING		ADMITTED		TO C.C.S		TO C.R.S		TO C.S.S		DUTY		DIED		REMAINING	
	O	O.R	O	O.R	O	O.R	O	O.R	O	O.R	O	O.R	O	O.R	O	O.R
8th		18										3				15
20th		4														4
35th		197	2	25	2	10		14				9				189
40th		52	4	14	4	6		4				4				52
42nd		227	1	40	1	18		22				14				213
59th	1	130	1	16	2	12		9				9				116
Ochu.Formation		102		18		10		6				5				99
	1	730	8	113	9	56		55				44				688

III(rd) Corps Main Dressing Station. Daily Sick States.

From 12/6/17 to 13/6/17.

DIVISION	REMAINING		ADMITTED		TO CAS. CLG. STA.		TO CORPS REST STA.		TO CORPS SCABIES STA.		DUTY		DIED		REMAINING	
	O	O.R	O	O.R	O	O.R	O	O.R	O	O.R	O	O.R	O	O.R	O	O.R
8th		15				1						2				12
20th		4														4
35th		189	2	38	2	17		34				7				169
40th		52		10		2		4				5				51
42nd		213		17		6		39				13				172
59th		116	1	52	1	6		15				9				138
Other Formations		99	1	33	1	11		7				7				107
		688	4	150	4	43		99				43				653

From 13/6/17 to 14/6/17.

DIVISION	REMAINING		ADMITTED		TO C.C.S		TO C.R.S		TO C.S.S		DUTY		DIED		REMAINING	
	O	O.R	O	O.R	O	O.R	O	O.R	O	O.R	O	O.R	O	O.R	O	O.R
8th		12														12
20th		4														4
35th		169	2	38	2	16		4				7				180
40th		51		10		5		3								53
42nd		172	3	37	3	22		4				5				178
59th		138	2	23	1	18		4				8			1	131
Other Formations		107	1	10		10		4				9			1	94
		653	8	118	6	71		19				29			2	652

From 14/6/17 to 15/6/17.

DIVISION	REMAINING		ADMITTED		TO C.C.S		TO C.R.S		TO C.S.S		DUTY		DIED		REMAINING	
	O	O.R	O	O.R	O	O.R	O	O.R	O	O.R	O	O.R	O	O.R	O	O.R
8th		12														12
20th		4														4
35th		180		7		38		24				5				120
40th		53	1	18	1	16		8				1				46
42nd		178	1	37	1	32		23				19				141
59th	1	131	2	22	1	30		13			1	6			1	104
Other Formations		94	2	20	3	21		9				10				74
	2	652	6	104	6	137		77			1	41			1	501

III rd Corps Main Dressing Station. Daily Sick States

From 15/6/17 to 16/6/17

DIVISION	REMAINING		ADMITTED		TO CAS CLG STA		TO CORPS REST STA		DUTY		DIED		REMAINING	
	O	O.R	O	O.R	O	O.R	O	O.R	O	O.R	O	O.R	O	O.R
8th		12								1				11
20th		4				1								3
35th		120		4		11		18		6				89
40th		46		17		24		6		2				31
42nd		141	1	29	1	23		24		7				116
59th	1	104	2	22	1	20		16		5			2	86
Other Formations		74		15		13		11		10				55
Germans				1		1								
	1	501	3	88	2	92		75		31			2	391

From 16/6/17 to 17/6/17

DIVISION	REMAINING		ADMITTED		TO C.C.S		TO C.R.S		DUTY		DIED		REMAINING	
	O	O.R	O	O.R	O	O.R	O	O.R	O	O.R	O	O.R	O	O.R
8th		11												11
20th		3												3
35th		89	3	36	3	13		11		7				94
40th		31	2	17	2	12		5						31
42nd		116	4	40	3	19		11		4				121
59th	2	86	2	24	3	13		9	1	3		1		85
Other Formations		55		15		8		6		2				54
	2	391	11	132	11	65		42	1	16		1	1	399

From 17/6/17 to 18/6/17

DIVISION	REMAINING		ADMITTED		TO C.C.S		TO C.R.S		DUTY		DIED		REMAINING	
	O	O.R	O	O.R	O	O.R	O	O.R	O	O.R	O	O.R	O	O.R
8th		11								1				10
20th		3						1						2
35th		94		29		18		11		2				92
40th		31	1	20	1	18		5						28
42nd		121	1	53	1	20		17		1		1		135
59th	1	85		33		15		19	1	5				79
Other Formations		54	1	15	1	13		11		5				40
	1	399	3	150	3	84		64	1	14		1		386

III rd Corps Main Dressing Station Daily Sick States

From 18/6/17 to 19/6/17.

DIVISION	REMAINING		ADMITTED		CAS TO CLG STA		TO CORPS REST TA				DUTY		DIED		REMAINING	
	O	O.R.	O	O.R.	O	O.R	O	O.R	O	O.R	O	O.R	O	O.R	O	O.R
8th		10										1				9
20th		2														2
35th		92	4	46	4	30		10				6				92
40th		28		14		12		2				2		1		25
42nd		135	1	33	1	22		14				5		1		126
59th		79	1	27	1	22		8				1				75
Attd Tomas		40		16		12		1				3				40
		386	6	136	6	98		35				18		2		369

From 19/6/17 to 20/6/17.

DIVISION	REMAINING		ADMITTED		TO C.C.S.		TO C.R.S				DUTY		DIED		REMAINING	
	O	O.R.	O	O.R.	O	O.R	O	O.R	O	O.R	O	O.R	O	O.R	O	O.R
8th		9														9
20th		2														2
35th		92	1	25	1	21						3				93
40th		25		10		10										25
42nd		126	3	35	3	26						3				132
59th		75	1	22	1	20						4				73
Attd Tomas		40		10		11						4				35
		369	5	102	5	88						14				369

From 20/6/17 to 21/6/17.

DIVISION	REMAINING		ADMITTED		TO C.C.S.		TO C.R.S				DUTY		DIED		REMAINING	
	O	O.R.	O	O.R.	O	O.R	O	O.R	O	O.R	O	O.R	O	O.R	O	O.R
8th		9										1				8
20th		2														2
35th		93	1	23	1	26		27				8				55
40th		25		23		21		6				1				20
42nd		132	1	41	1	51		32				10				80
59th		73		17		30		20				4				36
Attd Formation		35		20		20		5				2				28
		369	2	124	2	148		90				26				229

III rd Corps Main Dressing Station. Daily Sick States.

From 21/6/17 to 22/6/17.

DIVISION	REMAINING		ADMITTED		CAS TO CLG STA		TO CORPS REST STA				DUTY		DIED		REMAINING	
	O	O.R	O	O.R	O	O.R	O	O.R	O	O.R	O	O.R	O	O.R	Officers	Other Ranks
8th		8														8
20th		2										1				1
35th		55	1	21	1	12		13				6		1		44
40th		20	3	7	3	6		5				3				13
42nd		80		39		28		14				7				70
59th		36	2	22	2	10		3				3				42
Other Formation		28		17		13		4				5				23
		229	6	106	6	69		39				25		1		201

From 22/6/17 to 23/6/17.

DIVISION	REMAINING		ADMITTED		CAS TO CLG STA		TO CORPS REST STA				DUTY		DIED		REMAINING	
	O	O.R	O	O.R	O	O.R	O	O.R	O	O.R	O	O.R	O	O.R	O	O.R
8th		8														8
20th		1														1
35th		44	1	13	1	10		9				1				37
40th		13	1	18		16		4						1		11
42nd		70	2	32	2	36		2								64
59th		42	2	8	2	12		6								32
Other Formation		23		9		12		1				1				18
		201	6	80	5	86		22				2		1		171

From 23/6/17 to 24/6/17.

DIVISION	REMAINING		ADMITTED		CAS TO CLG STA		TO CORPS REST STA				DUTY		DIED		REMAINING	
	O	O.R	O	O.R	O	O.R	O	O.R	O	O.R	O	O.R	O	O.R	O	O.R
8th		8														8
20th		1														1
35th		37	1	14	1	10										41
40th	1	11	2	13	2	11									1	13
42nd		64		28		29						1				62
59th		32		16		14						2				32
Other Formation		18		10		7						3				18
	1	171	3	81	3	71						6			1	175

III rd Corps Main Dressing Station. Daily Sick States.

From 24/6/17 to 25/6/17

DIVISION	REMAINING		ADMITTED		CAS TO CLG STA		TO CORPS REST STA				DUTY		DIED		REMAINING	
	O	O.R.	O	O.R.	O	O.R.	O	O.R.	O	O.R.	O	O.R.	O	O.R.	O	O.R.
8th		8														8
20th		1														1
35th		41	1	25	1	17		7								42
40th	1	13	1	7		7		1							1	12
42nd		62		40		28		1								73
59th		32	1	8	1	6		3								31
Corps Formation		18		9		6		2				1				18
	1	175	3	89	3	64		14				1			1	185

From 25/6/17 to 26/6/17

DIVISION	REMAINING		ADMITTED		CAS TO CLG STA		TO CORPS REST STA				DUTY		DIED		REMAINING	
	O	O.R.	O	O.R.	O	O.R.	O	O.R.	O	O.R.	O	O.R.	O	O.R.	O	O.R.
8th		8										8				
20th		1														1
35th		42	1	15	1	14						1				42
40th	1	12		29		23		1								18
42nd		73	1	21	1	29						6				59
59th		31	2	14	2	9						2				34
Corps Formation		18		14		7										25
	1	185	4	93	4	82	1					17				179

From 26/6/17 to 27/6/17

DIVISION	REMAINING		ADMITTED		TO C.C.S.		TO C.R.S.				DUTY		DIED		REMAINING	
	O	O.R.	O	O.R.	O	O.R.	O	O.R.	O	O.R.	O	O.R.	O	O.R.	O	O.R.
8th																
20th		1														1
35th		42	1	14		9									1	47
40th		18	1	19	1	10										27
42nd		59		26		23										62
59th		34	1	3	1	3						1				33
Corps Formation		25	1	10	1	9						1				25
		179	4	72	3	54						2			1	195

III rd Corps Main Dressing Station. Daily Sick States

From 27/6/17 to 28/6/17

DIVISION	REMAINING		ADMITTED		TO CAS. CLG STA		TO CORPS REST STA				DUTY		DIED		REMAINING	
	O	O.R	O	O.R	O	O.R	O	O.R	O	O.R	O	O.R	O	O.R	O	O.R
20th		1														1
35th	1	47		19	1	11		11						1		43
40th		27	1	16	1	10		5								28
42nd		62		13		11		17								47
59th		33	3	8	3	7		4				1				29
Other Formations		25		7		2		9								21
	1	195	4	63	5	41		46				1		1		169

From 28/6/17 to 29/6/17

DIVISION	REMAINING		ADMITTED		TO C.C.S		TO C.R.S				DUTY		DIED		REMAINING	
	O	O.R	O	O.R	O	O.R	O	O.R	O	O.R	O	O.R	O	O.R	O	O.R
20th		1														1
35th		43	1	7	1	6						2				42
40th		28	1	18	1	19										27
42nd		47		30		3						1		3		70
59th		29		19		7						1				40
Other Formations		21		6		4										23
		169	2	80	2	39						4		3		203

From 29/6/17 to 30/6/17

DIVISION	REMAINING		ADMITTED		TO C.C.S		TO C.R.S				DUTY		DIED		REMAINING	
	O	O.R	O	O.R	O	O.R	O	O.R	O	O.R	O	O.R	O	O.R	O	O.R
20th		1														1
35th		42		20		11		8				1				42
40th		27		18		14		5								26
42nd		70	2	85		77		10				1		3	1	65
59th		40	3	17	3	9		5								43
Other Formations		23	1	14	1	11		2				2				22
German Prisoners				1		1										
		203	6	155	4	123		30				3	1	3	1	199

Confidential.

No 18

War Diary

of

105th Field Ambulance R.A.M.C

From

1st July 1917

to

31st July 1917.

Inclusive

Volume XVIII   Original

WAR DIARY
or
INTELLIGENCE SUMMARY
(Erase heading not required.)

Army Form C. 2118

Instructions regarding War Diaries and Intelligence Summaries are contained in F. S. Regs., Part II. and the Staff Manual respectively. Title Pages will be prepared in manuscript.

Place	Date	Hour	Summary of Events and Information	Remarks and references to Appendices
III C M D S FINS	1.7.17		1 NCO and 12 men, 12 men W/goers detailed for duty at Cmcl Hospital PERONNE	97 H
"	2.7.17		Lieut A.B. MacCARTHY R.A.M.C proceeded to Cmcl Hospital PERONNE for duty	97 H
"	3.7.17		Nothing to report	97 H
"	4.7.17		63567 Sgt KNIGHT J. proceeded to attend a Course of instruction at 3.5.E. Divisional Gas School	97 H
"	4.7.17		Three Ambulance and two Fords returned from 106 Field Ambulance	97 H
"	5.7.17		3 NCO's and 17 men proceeded to Cmcl Hospital PERONNE for duty	97 H
"	6.7.17		6098 Sgt D.J McAFEE R.A.M.C granted leave from 6.7.17 to 16.7.17	97 H
"	6.7.17		The u/m men were presented with Rewards (Military Medal) by III Corps Commander:— 63916 Pte TODD. J ⎱ R.A.M.C S.0995 " BOWERS T.W ⎰	97 H
"	7.7.17		Fatigue Party 1 NCO and 10 men returned to 2/3 West MIDLAND Field Ambulance. 1 Sergt Clerk returned to 1/1st E. LANCS Field Ambulance & 3 thirds returned to 1/1st E. LANCS Field Ambulance	97 H
"	8.7.17		1 NCO and 4 men proceeded to take on Both. at ST EMILIE	97 H
"	8.9.17		1 NCO and 2 men proceeded to take on Both at EPEHY	
"	8.7.17		2 Ambulance Cars and 17 men attached to 107 Field Ambulance for duty	97 H

WAR DIARY or **INTELLIGENCE SUMMARY**
(Erase heading not required.)

Army Form C. 2118

Instructions regarding War Diaries and Intelligence Summaries are contained in F. S. Regs., Part II. and the Staff Manual respectively. Title Pages will be prepared in manuscript.

Place	Date	Hour	Summary of Events and Information	Remarks and references to Appendices
III C.M.D.S. FINS	9/7/17		The u/m men posted to 105" Field Ambulance and taken on the strength accordingly:- 338205 Pte BRAITHAUPT G 367310 " DIXON W E 339207 " HAYWORTH G 367131 " LUND L H 357335 " ROBINSON B 375050 " TATLOW J M 347175 " THOMPSON J G 339166 " WALMSLEY A E 367369 " HART M	
"	9/7/17		Above 9 men posted to 107 Field Ambulance	47 H
"	10/7/17		105" Field Ambulance moved to LONGAVESNES leaving at 2.45 PM. Map reference FRANCE sheet 62c E 25 c 5 8. All patients (2 officers 195 O.R.) transferred to incoming unit (136 Field Ambulance)	47 H
LONGAVESNES	10/7/17		Established Divisional Rest Station at LONGAVESNES (received north B. ech. taken over from 107 Field Ambulance)	47 H
"	11/7/17		Nothing to report	47 H
"	12/7/17		12 men proceeded for duty with 3.5." Divisional Hy Artillery	47 H

WAR DIARY
or
INTELLIGENCE SUMMARY

(Erase heading not required.)

Army Form C. 2118

Instructions regarding War Diaries and Intelligence Summaries are contained in F. S. Regs., Part II. and the Staff Manual respectively. Title Pages will be prepared in manuscript.

Place	Date	Hour	Summary of Events and Information	Remarks and references to Appendices
LONGUENESSE	13.7.17		nothing to report	47 H
"	14.7.17		nothing to report	47 H
"	15.7.17		nothing to report	47 H
"	16.7.17		Capt T.F. HEGARTY RAMC transferred from No 5 CCS to 105 Field Ambulance vice Lt Col G.H. RICHARD RAMC promoted	47 H
"	17.7.17		nothing to report	47 H
"	18.7.17		nothing to report	47 H
"	19.7.17		nothing to report	47 H
"	20.7.17		Units inspected by D.D.M.S. III Corps	47 H
"	21.7.17		nothing to report	47 H
"	22.7.17		nothing to report	47 H
"	23.7.17		nothing to report	47 H
"	24.7.17		nothing to report	47 H
"	25.7.17		Lt Col Ant Duncan attached to 56 C.C.S for duty Capt W.J. SCADE RAMC (T.F) posted to 105 Field Ambulance vice Capt dis duty men attached to 56th Division reported. They return respective 105 Field Ambulance men strength accordingly	47 H

WAR DIARY
or
INTELLIGENCE SUMMARY

(Erase heading not required.)

Army Form C. 2118

Instructions regarding War Diaries and Intelligence Summaries are contained in F.S. Regs., Part II and the Staff Manual respectively. Title Pages will be prepared in manuscript.

Place	Date	Hour	Summary of Events and Information	Remarks and references to Appendices
LONGAVESNES	26.7.17		Capt W J SCADE RAMC (TF) proceeded for duty with 19th HIGHLAND LIGHT INF. and struck off strength	7 7 H
"	27.7.17		Lieut A R HILL RAMC proceeded for duty as M.O. 1/c 14th GLOSTER REGT to relieve Lieut WHITE RAMC.	7 7 H
"			No 90546 (A/Sgt OFFER R J returned from III Corps demonstration Aug ??)	7 7 H
"	28.7.17		Nothing to report	7 7 H
"	29.7.17		Nothing to report	7 7 H
"	30.7.17		90464 Staff Sgt HAY A proceeded to III Corps demonstration depot to replace Sgt OFFER R J	7 7 H
"	31.7.17		Nothing to report	7 7 H

III Corps Main Dressing Station. Daily Sick States

From 30/6/17 to 1/7/17

DIVISION	Remained		Admtd		To CCS		To CRS		Duty		Died		Remaining	
	O	OR	O	OR	O	OR	O	OR	O	OR	O	OR	O	OR
20th		1												1
35th		42		29		13		9				4		45
40th		26	1	14		8		3					1	29
42nd	1	65		25		12		11			1	1		66
59th		43		12		13		5				3		34
Other Formation		22		6		5		3						20
Germans				1		1								
	1	199	2	86	1	51		31				8	2	195

From 1/7/17 to 2/7/17

DIVISION	Remained		Admtd		To CCS		To CRS		Duty		Died		Remaining	
	O	OR	O	OR	O	OR	O	OR	O	OR	O	OR	O	OR
20th		1												1
35th		45	2	22	1	15		14	1					38
40th	1	29		6	1	6		7						21
42nd	1	66		11		6		3					1	68
59th		34	2	4	2	3		1						34
Other Formation		20		6		4		2						20
Germans														
	2	195	4	49	4	34		27	1				1	182

From 2/7/17 to 3/7/17

DIVISION	Remained		Admtd		To CCS		To CRS		Duty		Died		Remaining	
	O	OR	O	OR	O	OR	O	OR	O	OR	O	OR	O	OR
20th		1												1
35th		38		34		15		7				1		49
40th		21	1	11	1	12		2		1				17
42nd	1	68		23		21		2					1	68
59th		34		14		13		1						34
Other Formation		20		6		6		1		1				18
	1	182	1	88	1	67		13		2		1	1	187

IIIrd Corps Main Dressing Station. Daily Sick States.

From 3/7/17 to 4/7/17

DIVISION	Remained		Admitted		to C.C.S		to C.R.S		Duty		Died		Remaining	
	O	O.R	O	O.R	O	O.R	O	O.R	O	O.R	O	O.R	O	O.R
20th		1												1
35th		49	1	1		2								47
40th		17	1	14	1	14						1		16
42nd	1	68	1	15	1	5						1	1	77
59th		34		10		5				1				38
Other Formation		18		8		3				1				22
	1	187	3	47	3	29				2		2	1	201

From 4/7/17 to 5/7/17

DIVISION	Remained		Admitted		to C.C.S		to C.R.S		Duty		Died		Remaining	
	O	O.R	O	O.R	O	O.R	O	O.R	O	O.R	O	O.R	O	O.R
20th		1												1
35th		47	1	16	1	3		9						51
40th		16	2	36	2	24		5						23
42nd	1	77		29		15		6		2			1	83
59th		38		17		10		2						43
Other Formation		22		14		7		1						28
German				1		1								
	1	201	3	113	3	60		23		2			1	229

From 5/7/17 to 6/7/17

DIVISION	Remained		Admitted		to C.C.S		to C.R.S		Duty		Died		Remaining	
	O	O.R	O	O.R	O	O.R	O	O.R	O	O.R	O	O.R	O	O.R
20th		1												1
35th		51		22		15		6		3				49
40th		23	4	29	4	23		1		3		2		23
42nd	1	83		43	1	59		7						60
59th		43	3	16	3	16		3						40
Other Formation		28	1	13	1	12		3		2				24
	1	229	8	123	9	125		20		8		2		197

III.rd Corps Main Dressing Station. Daily Sick State

From 6/7/17 to 7/7/17

DIVISION	Remained		Admitted		to C.C.S		to C.R.S		Duty		Died		Remaining	
	O	OR	O	OR	O	OR	O	OR	O	OR	O	OR	O	OR
20th		1												1
35th		49		1		2								48
40th		23	2	31	1	15				2		1		37
42nd		60		22		18				1				63
59th		40		11		8				1				42
Other Formation		24		21		10								35
		197	2	86	1	53				4		1		226

From 7/7/17 to 8/7/17

DIVISION	Remained		Admitted		to C.C.S		to C.R.S		Duty		Died		Remaining	
	O	OR	O	OR	O	OR	O	OR	O	OR	O	OR	O	OR
20th		1								1				
35th		48				2				12				34
40th	1	37	4	38	4	27				3		1		46
42nd		63		45		15				17		1		75
59th		42	1	23	1	21				7		1		36
Other Formation		35		17		10				6				36
	1	226	5	123	5	75				46		2	1	226

From 8/7/17 to 9/7/17

DIVISION	Remained		Admitted		to C.C.S		to C.R.S		Duty		Died		Remaining	
	O	OR	O	OR	O	OR	O	OR	O	OR	O	OR	O	OR
20th														
35th		34	3	17	2	6						1	1	44
40th	1	46		47	1	36				1				55
42nd		75		3		10				1				67
59th		36	1	2	1	9								29
Other Formation		36	1	2	1	5				1				32
	1	226	5	71	5	66				3		1	1	227

IIIrd Corps Main Dressing Station. Daily Sick State.

From 9/7/19 to 10/7/19

DIVISION	Remained		Admitted		To C.C.S.		To C.R.S.		To Duty		Died		Remaining	
	O	OR	O	OR	O	OR	O	OR	O	OR	O	OR	O	OR
20th														
35th	1	44	1	9	1	12				2			1	39
40th		55	2	29	1	32				4			1	48
42nd		67	1	3	1	7				1				62
59th		29		2		2				11				18
Other Formation		32	1	8	1	7				2				31
	1	227	5	51	4	60				20			2	198

All patients transferred to 136 Field Ambulance on this Unit leaving the IIIrd Corps Main Dsg Sta.

Confidential

War Diary

of

105th Field Ambulance R.A.M.C.

From

1st August 1917.

to

31st August 1917.

Inclusive.

Volume XIX   Original

Army Form C. 2118

WAR DIARY
or
INTELLIGENCE SUMMARY   105 Field Ambulance

(Erase heading not required.)

Instructions regarding War Diaries and Intelligence Summaries are contained in F. S. Regs., Part II. and the Staff Manual respectively. Title Pages will be prepared in manuscript.

Place	Date	Hour	Summary of Events and Information	Remarks and references to Appendices
LONGAVESNES	1/8/17 2/8/17		LIEUT. A.B. MACARTHY & 4 men rejoined The Unit from Civil HOSPITAL PERONNE. The undermentioned N.C.O. re-joined hqrs the Unit. he details will appear in 29/7/17. 63672 L/Cpl TAAFFE. T	
	3/8/17		Nothing to report	
	4/8/17		The undermentioned Officers posted to 105 Field AMBULANCE & taken on the strength Capt J.E. PEARCE R.A.M.C. T.F. " S.R. GLEED R.A.M.C.	
	5/8/17		Nothing to report	
	6/8/17		Capt C SCAIFE R.A.M.C. posted to 105 Field Ambulance and previous command from	
	7/8/17		This day. Lieut A.B. MACARTHY detailed as Officer i/c Medical Duties Lieut R.J. HELSBY R.A.M.C. proceeded for duty as Regt Med Officer to 20th Lancs. F.& L. Struck off the strength accordingly. Capt G.W. LLOYD R.A.M.C. (T.C.) posted to 105 F.A.	
	8/8/17		& taken on strength R. Unit Capt G.W. LLOYD is detailed as Officer i/c at LONGAVESNES & STEMILIE op hrs	
	9/8/17		62 C E 24 A.S.S Capt E. PHILLIPS. M.C. R.A.M.C. rejoined R. Unit	
	10/8/17		Lieut R.R. MacCARTHY R.A.M.C. proceeded for temporary duty as M.O. i/c W.A.Cops Eyelet Camp. 5 cases admitted Hq cases remaining	

WAR DIARY or INTELLIGENCE SUMMARY

Army Form C. 2118

Place	Date	Hour	Summary of Events and Information	Remarks and references to Appendices
LONGAVESNES	11/VII/17.		Lt. A.R. HILL who proceeded to duty as M.O. 'C' 14 Gloucester Regt on 25th ult. is still sick of strength. Batln at ST EMILIE unposted.	S.P
			9 cases admitted 75 cases reviewing	S.P
	12/VII/17		11 " 82 "	S.P
	13		6 " 79 "	S.P/12
	14		3 " 77 "	S.P/12
	15		7 " 72 "	
	16		3 " 61 "	
	17		10 " 67 "	
	18/VII/17.		52 O.R. 3 Horseguns & 1 N.C.O proceeded for duty with 107 F.A Capt. Hare atta R.M.C. attached to 107 F.A. for temporary duty.	S.P
			4 cases admitted 61 cases reviewing	
	19/VII/17.		Capts Lloyd Pierce proceeded at 5 a.m. to 107 F.A to avoid ill-treatment of wounded from German Town attack. They returned at 1 P.m. after assisting them. Batln at ST EMILIE unposted. 107 F.A marked at VILLERS FAUCON. 20 cases admitted 72 cases reviewing	S.P
	20/VII/17.		Orders received for return of Capt Hareafter minimum leave. One one of Rose measles evacuated to 38 C.C.S. Orders received for Capt Pierce to proceed to 19 C.C.S. to temporary duty. Capt. Geers detailed for duty as M.O. 'C' 18 Cheshire in 23rd unit. Capt Haggerty 28 S.R.	

WAR DIARY
or
INTELLIGENCE SUMMARY
(Erase heading not required.)

Army Form C. 2118

Place	Date	Hour	Summary of Events and Information	Remarks and references to Appendices
LONGAVESNES	20th		All units of unit inspected by D.A.D.V.S. at VILLERS FAUCON. Capt MCAFEE returned to Ambulance from temp'y duty with 107M. 12 cases admitted 84 cases remaining	SP
	21.		Order received for Capt PEARCE to proceed for Temp'y duty at 19 C.C.S. " " M.O. to relieve M.O. 1/2 16 Cheshires in 2.3.D.	SP
			with Capt GEED detailed 6 cases admitted 76 cases remaining.	SP
	22		1 N.C.O. + 12 men returned from Civil Hospital PERONNE. been from billets at EPEHY + ST EMILE rejoined unit in relief by 107 F.A. Orders received for one section of ambulance to proceed to C.R.S MOISLAINS 9 cases admitted 80 cases remaining	SP
	23D		A.D.M.S. inspected ambulance. Capt GEED proceeded to 16 Cheshires to relieve M.O. proceeding on leave. One reser +2 G.S. wagons with Capts McAFEE + LLOYD proceeded to CRS MOISLAINS 3 cases admitted 76 remaining	SP

WAR DIARY or INTELLIGENCE SUMMARY

Army Form C. 2118

Place	Date	Hour	Summary of Events and Information	Remarks and references to Appendices
LONGAVESNES	24	2pm	Civil Hospital PERONNE inspected + men here paid	
		6pm	Orders received for another N.C.O. + two men sent to III CCS	
		7pm	Visited A.D.M.S. + discussed construction of baths, shelters + places of winter hutting. 79 cases remaining. 5 cases admitted	S.P.
	25.		Capt HEGARTY + 27 O.R. granted 10 days leave	
		9.0am	Orders received from M.D.M.S. to dispatch 2 Forrest rugs car to A.D.S. 107 L'EMPIRE. 63 remaining. 2 cases admitted	S.P.
	26.		Hutting forms. 18 cases admitted. 69 remaining	S.P.
	27		Heavy rain interfered with outdoor work. Sites for winter hutting fixed. One men dispatched to attend Field Army School of Cookery. 12 cases admitted. 75 remaining	
	28		Chief duties: M.D.M.S. visited. Ambulance inspected. Sites for erection of huts for winter. 79 cases remaining. 6 cases admitted	

WAR DIARY
or
INTELLIGENCE SUMMARY

(Erase heading not required.)

Army Form C. 2118

Place	Date	Hour	Summary of Events and Information	Remarks and references to Appendices
LONGUEVESNES	29.		Work commenced on new horse standings & clearing out old stables. Work much delayed by bad weather. 4 cases admitted. 77 cases remaining.	S.P.
	30		L/A.B. McCARTHY reported sick from divine duty as M.O. to 2nd Cps. Cyclist Batn. 4 cases admitted. 69 remaining.	S.P.
	31.		Warning order received to prepare for drawing 10 horses huts to write quarters of D.R.S. 6 cases admitted. 70 cases remaining.	S.P.

John Richsh Cushenna

for O.C, 105TH Field Amb. ANZC

<u>Confidential</u>

<u>War Diary</u>
– of –
<u>105th Field Ambulance. R.A.M.C.</u>

<u>From</u>
<u>1st September 1917.</u>
– to –
<u>30th September 1917</u>
<u>Inclusive</u>

<u>Volume XX</u> <u>Original.</u>

Confidential

War Diary

— of —

105th Field Ambulance. R.A.M.C.

From

1st September 1917

— to —

30th September 1917.

Inclusive.

Volume XX   Original.

WAR DIARY
or
INTELLIGENCE SUMMARY
(Erase heading not required.)

Army Form C. 2118

Place	Date	Hour	Summary of Events and Information	Remarks and references to Appendices
LONGAVESNES	1.IX.17		All personnel employed in constructing work in camp. Horse huts drawn from TINCOURT for winter. D.Sr. Rob. Sh. work on stables commenced. 6 cases admitted. 68 cases remaining.	SP
	2.IX.17		Work delayed by weather. A.D.M.S. visited hospital today. 4 cases admitted. 64 cases remaining.	SP
	3.IX.17		8 cases admitted. 67 " "	SP
	4.IX.17		Nothing to report. 2 cases admitted. 67 " "	SP
	5.IX.17		14 O.R. proceeded on leave today from ROISEL. 13 cases admitted. 76 cases remaining.	SP
	6.IX.17		Lt MEAD reported for duty. Capt LLOYD rejoined from duty temp duty @ 53 C.C.S. 14 O.R. proceeded on leave today. 7 cases admitted. 76 cases remaining.	SP
	7.IX.17		29 O.R. rejoined from leave. Capt HEGATY rejoined from leave. A.D.M.S visited hospital + camp. 5 cases admitted. 81 cases remaining.	SP

WAR DIARY
INTELLIGENCE SUMMARY
(Erase heading not required.)

Army Form C. 2118

Place	Date	Hour	Summary of Events and Information	Remarks and references to Appendices
	8		T/12240 S/SSM. HOOVER A.E.C. promoted S.S.M. for duration of war with effect from May 2nd. 77 cases reviewing. 1 case admitted	SP
	9		Capt. HEGATY proceeded to PERONNE to relieve Capt. MATHEWS ½- Civil Hospital. 3 cases admitted. 75 cases reviewing	SP
	10		10 A.S.C. hitmen replaced by 10 P.B. Personnel (Infantry): A.S.C. hitmen sent to 35 D.R. Train to evac. W. Base. 4 cases admitted. 78 cases reviewing	SP
	11		Lieut MEAD J.C. R.A.M.C. proceeded to Kilponey duty with 18th H.L.I. in absence of Capt. SCROPE on leave. 1 case admitted. 77 cases reviewing. 2 cases admitted. 73 cases reviewing	SP
	12 13		Capt. LLOYD. G.W. R.A.M.C. proceeded to England in expiration of contract	SP
	13		Lieut MEAD, J.C. R.A.M.C. rejoined from 18.14.61. 5 cases admitted. 75 cases reviewing	SP
	14		Hon. Qm. Tynan granted leave until 24.5. 3 cases admitted. 75 cases reviewing	SP

WAR DIARY
or
INTELLIGENCE SUMMARY
(Erase heading not required.)

Army Form C. 2118

Place	Date	Hour	Summary of Events and Information	Remarks and references to Appendices
	15th		Lieut J.C. MEAD proceeded for temporary duty with 61 C.C.S. 4 cases admitted 79 cases remaining	SP
	16th		nothing to report 3 cases admitted 73 cases remaining	SP
	17		horses huts being erected, walls in batten plated. Scales partially completed, pine stove boxes for 3 horse stables constructed. 5 cases admitted 77 cases remaining	SP
	18th		Lieut E.B. PEASE M.O.R.C. U.S.A. posted hitherto unit for duty. SP A.D.M.S. visited unit, inspected unit. 10 cases admitted 82 cases remaining	SP
	19th		Lieut MEAD transferred to 47 C.C.S. for permanent duty Work carried on with units hutting, stoves, drainage. 5 cases admitted 80 cases remaining	SP
	20th 20		Lieut M.D. MacCARTHY proceeded for duty with IIIrd Cps School SP Huaspinch 5th Chiwata D.D.M.S. visited unit. 9 cases admitted 78 cases remaining	SP
	21st		18 cases admitted 95 " remaining	SP

WAR DIARY or INTELLIGENCE SUMMARY

Army Form C. 2118

Date	Hour	Summary of Events and Information	Remarks and references to Appendices
22nd		Work continued in erection of winter shelters huts. 5 new huts now completed & 8 now in course of erection. 6 cases admitted. 57 cases remaining.	P.P.
23rd		C.R.E. 35 Div. visited unit & enquired about progress with hutting with view planting. Authority obtained to erect 2 new huts now having a total of 20 huts. 12 cases admitted. 64 cases remaining.	P.P.
24	10.45am	Transport (H.T.) inspected by O.C. 35 Div. Train. Lieut PEARCE M.O.R.C. U.S.A. instructed by H.Q. 1/c 14 F.A. in duties of R.M.O. 7 cases admitted. 72 cases remaining.	P.P.
25th		Hospital buildings and patients transferred to new site at Longevesnes. 18 cases admitted. 88 cases remaining.	P.P.
26th		Field Service granted leave until 7/10/17. Lieut PEARCE M.O.R.C. U.S.A proceeded to WEPENY D/D.S 106 F.A. for 24hrs instruction. 1 case admitted. 81 cases remaining.	P.P.
27th		Lieut Dyson rejoined unit from leave. Pte Johns G. 1st Sp. Convalescent Depot rejoined today. 1 case admitted. 49 cases remaining.	P.P.

Place	Date	Hour	Summary of Events and Information	Remarks and references to Appendices
LONGAVESNES	28/5 29.		5 cases admitted. 23 cases remaining. Ambulance waited mt loading our train Ambulance of SSS bis. Ambulance opened in PERONNE into 10a Inf Bde at 2 P.m. Civilian officer two units of '04 Rgt. concerned. 2 cases remaining. 1 case admitted.	
PERONNE	30.		Detached from III M CRS MOSLAINS + Civil Hospital PERONNE rejoined unit today. Capt Pearce doing duty at 14 C.C.S. was placed on strength of his unit. 2 cases remain. 1 case admitted.	

Ruut Capitaine
p. O.C. 105 D.A.

Confidential.

War Diary

of

105 Field Ambulance R.A.M.C.

From

1st October 1917.

to

31st October 1917.

Inclusive.

Volume XXI   Original.

WAR DIARY
or
INTELLIGENCE SUMMARY
(Erase heading not required.)

Army Form C. 2118

Place	Date	Hour	Summary of Events and Information	Remarks and references to Appendices
PERONNE	1/X/16		Field Ambulance "resting". Detachment from 55 C.C.S. + party under Capt. HEGARTY @ CIVIL HOSPITAL rejoined today. Lt & Q.M. Tyson proceeded to new area for billeting.	
	2/X/17	6.0am	Transport under Capt. MACAFEE proceeded with F.T. of B⁴ group by march route to BAPAUME, where detachment halted.	
		12.30pm	12 O.R. (water cart) en route to BAPAUME, 8 miles east to AUBIGNY	
		1.0 pm	M.T. proceeded in convoy to LATTRE ST QUENTIN via BAPAUME & ARRAS	
		9.30 pm	Remainder of unit proceeded by "Tactical train" to AUBIGNY. With ran assembled here; transport not yet arrived. Poor billets.	
LATTRE— ST QUENTIN near ARRAS.	3/X/17	9.00 am	With ran assembled here with very little hospital accommodation.	
		12.0 pm	Transport arrived by road; all transport reported safely.	
		2.0 pm	A.D.M.S. visited site then proceeded to WAGNONS to inspect old ambulance site there. A very excellent place. Orders received from A.D.M.S. to prepare knew lines in L.T.	
		7.0 pm	185/FWV/16/26 1.5 OMound V.E. Sewage Eft./Forth/1.18. proceeded to VETINES in L.T. + receive	

WAR DIARY or INTELLIGENCE SUMMARY

Army Form C. 2118

Place	Date	Hour	Summary of Events and Information	Remarks and references to Appendices
AVESNES LE COMTE	4/X/17	9.0 am	Ambulance received from LATTRE ST QUENTIN & AUGSINES & relieved detachment of 38 F.A. at old C.C.S. site. Very excellent hutts accommodation obtained. Day spent in cleaning tidying up Hospital preparing for patients. A.D.M.S. visited ambulance.	SP
	5/X/17		Sick collected from units of Bde Group. Field Ambulance training SP undertaken, stretcher exercises, enfany physical dill work & training continues but owing to rain it is greatly hampered.	SP
	6/X/17			SP
	7/X/17		White line adopted night 6/7 Orders received for instructions between rear details men of units on leave to rejoin. Medical Board assembled to examine Cpl DYE —	SP
	8/X/17	10 am	Collection of sick continued. Training of unit continued. All to-night cleared up + wagon lines overhauled. Orders received Med A/Bing would report unit training 9.	SP

WAR DIARY
or
INTELLIGENCE SUMMARY
(Erase heading not required.)

Army Form C. 2118

Place	Date	Hour	Summary of Events and Information	Remarks and references to Appendices
AVEINES LE COMTE	9/X/17	10am	Complete field Ambulance inspected by M.O.'s today. Weather fine. Pte. MS Lin inspected to hospital.	SP
WAR ARRAS.		7pm	L/Cpl SEDIFE rejoined from leave.	
	10/X/17		nothing of which	SP / SP
	11/X/17		" "	
	12/X/17		Orders received for unit to proceed to ESQUELBECQ on 13th. Capt HERRITY ½ billeting party left today.	SP
	13/X/17	12noon	O.C. proceeded with all motor ambulances of Div. to BARNETÉ.	
		2/pm	H.T. marched to AUBIGNY to entraining.	SP
		8pm	Dismounted personnel proceeded to AUBIGNY to entrain.	SP
ZEGGARD CAPEL Lunt. Nr PSTEL	14/X/17	12.30am	Train left AUBIGNY arrived ETQUES BELG 6.0am + marches to CAPEL. Billets @ ZEGGERS CAPEL.	SP

1875 Wt. W593/826 1,000,000 4/15 J.B.C. & A. A.D.S.S./Forms/C. 2118.

WAR DIARY or INTELLIGENCE SUMMARY

Army Form C. 2118

Place	Date	Hour	Summary of Events and Information	Remarks and references to Appendices
15/X/17		11am	Ambulance entrained at ROUTELLE Mun, proceeded to PROVEN.	
		3pm	Detrained PROVEN marches to POPERINGHE Camp near CROMBEKE arriving about 4pm. (HAZEBROUCK Sh 2.1. 30 c 95)	
CROMBEKE	16th		Transport with Cookhouses proceeded by road. Cup & Sergts attached to 106 F.A. for duty.	Transfers to 14 Corps
		9pm	Capt. Wester Driver F.B. PEACE M.O.R.C. U.S.A. posted and proceeded for 1 T.S-D proceeded to No 46 C.C.S. for duty.	
"	17th		2 clerks attached to C.A.D.S. SOLFERINO + 1 to duty. Ambulance received at CROMBEKE.	
"	18th		No 4 F.A. Rlf at PROVEN visited in taking men. 2 N.C.O.s & 6 men proceeded into District in respirators. 8 clerks Laundry attached to duty at XIV Corps HQ.	
PROVEN	19th		Ambulance marched to PROVEN took over D.R.S. lines at 10 am from No 4 F.A.	

WAR DIARY
or
INTELLIGENCE SUMMARY

(Erase heading not required.)

Army Form C. 2118

Place	Date	Hour	Summary of Events and Information	Remarks and references to Appendices
PROVEN	20.5.		2 NCOs + 35 men of bearers S.D. attended T.O.O. P.A. for Fatigue duty	
	21st		2 ambulance cars proceeded for duty at OUST Fm. (106 F.A.) Two sheer detailed for duty retestiblished Rennes.	
	22nd		2 ambulance cars proceeded to 107 F.A. 15565 T.MN & DA Fm for duty	
	23rd		Ambulance at PROVEN with 3, 54 S.B. "incurables" Camps Hospital hut use C.E. Supply.	
	24th		2 NCOs + 28 men returned from 106 F.A.	
	25th		No 70891 Pte DAVIES E. Killed in 23rd inst. 5.O.R. wounded on 23rd & 24th	
			13 O.R. returned wounds from 106 F.A.	
	26		40 O.R. proceeded to duty C 106 F.A. No 68154 Pte WOOD G. Killed m 25th + 30 O.R. wounded	

Army Form C. 2118

WAR DIARY
or
INTELLIGENCE SUMMARY
(Erase heading not required.)

Place	Date	Hour	Summary of Events and Information	Remarks and references to Appendices
PROVEN	28th	2pm	Ambulance marched "in" and arrived 5.30pm. Preparation made for receiving patients.	
	29th		1 car proceeded for duty at XIV C.R.S. WORNHOUT.	
	30th		1 O.R. proceeded for duty at B/Fr Army School of Cookery. Lt. E.A. CHRISTOPHERSON, C.H. ARNOLD, A. MILTENBERGER, M.O.R.C., U.S.A. still to finish up duty.	
	31st		Whole ambulance fully employed in improving huts in camp. Playing trench-heads. Lectures.	

Rict Cipher
Lt Col RAMC
for 11/5 FA

Confidential

War Diary

of

105th Field Ambulance, R.A.M.C.

From

1st November 1917.

to

30th November 1917.

Inclusive.

Volume XXII   Original.

WAR DIARY
INTELLIGENCE SUMMARY

Army Form C. 2118

(Erase heading not required.)

Place	Date	Hour	Summary of Events and Information	Remarks and references to Appendices
"W" Camp A 7a central Sheet 28	1/X/17		Ambulances running DRS here. 2 O/rs detached for duty's @ 46 C.C.S. 1 O/r attached to 106 7.A.	
	2/X/17		HQ O.R. rejoined from attachment to 106 7.A.	
	3/X/17		Orders received to move to PURLEY Camp HARINGHE in s.e. corner m 56th 7.A. 18th Div. Head now recant. Taken over fm 56th 7.A. 56 7A site at	
	4/X/17		19 O.R. rejoined from attachment to 106 7.A. PURLEY CAMP visited.	
	5/X/17		6 O.R. evacuated to day gassed. 19 O.R. rejoined from Remy attachment to 06 7.A. 20 O.R. Transferred to XIV Corps.	
	6/X/17		Moved to PURLEY CAMP E 4 d 9.3 Sheet 27. T took over from 56 7A. 18th Div. wh ordered for all ranks	

WAR DIARY or INTELLIGENCE SUMMARY

Army Form C. 2118

(Erase heading not required.)

Instructions regarding War Diaries and Intelligence Summaries are contained in F.S. Regs, Part II. and the Staff Manual respectively. Title Pages will be prepared in manuscript.

Place	Date	Hour	Summary of Events and Information	Remarks and references to Appendices
PURLEY CAMP.	6/xi/17		MITTENBORGER, A. U.S.A. MRC proceeded for duty with 159 Bde R.F.A in relief of Lt Tinkle. 1 O.R. evacuated sick today.	
	7.xi.17		Ambulance parade at PROVEN with other ambulances of this Area. Were inspected here by Lt M.G. Cusgq. 1 O.R. evacuated today. Ambulance site at HERZEELE inspected today.	
HERZEELE	8.xi.17		5 O.R. proceeded for duty at 13 C.C.S. for relief of the Chungth. New Ambulance moved to HERZEELE Sheet 27. D8c 7.7 arriving at noon. 1 O.R. evacuated sick.	
	9.xi.17		1 S.R. reinforcement posted to us from Lieu puits today.	
	10.xi.17		Ambulance remains at HERZEELE. Reevers H/C (O/m) LEGATY proceeded in a motor truck	

WAR DIARY
or
INTELLIGENCE SUMMARY

(Erase heading not required.)

Army Form C. 2118

Place	Date	Hour	Summary of Events and Information	Remarks and references to Appendices
HERZEELE D8c77	11/xi/17		Sgt ANDERSON 54771 Cpl QUERATY 68193 L/Cpl TAAFFE 63901 Pte BROWN 63872 } awarded the Military Medal XIX C.R.O. 887	
	12/xi/17		Proceeded with A.D.M.S. 35 Div to visit A.D.M.S. 50 Div to make arrangements for taking over their front. O.C. of ambulances to be relieved interviewed. arrangements made with him for relief	
	13/xi/17		General routine work	
	14/xi/17			
	15/xi/17		Lt MITTENBORGER & 5 more rejoined Section on change Capt J.W. INNES came vice holt. Later unit for duty. 10th & 3 O.R. proceeded to 2/2 H.C. F.A. to arrange about relieving new A.D.Stn to him taken	

WAR DIARY
or
INTELLIGENCE SUMMARY
(Erase heading not required.)

Army Form C. 2118

Place	Date	Hour	Summary of Events and Information	Remarks and references to Appendices
HERZEELE	16/XI/17		Bearer Subs of A sub + 30 O.R. proceeded by lorry to ISLY Fm then took over A.D.S. MINTY Fm. C/O C 2·3 proceeded from 35th Brit Innf. Advance party came over ETSEX FM E ret'd S.S. as H.Q. 105 F.A.	
ESSEX F.M.	17/XI/17		Remainder of ambulance proceeded here relieved 2/2 HR F.A. Horse transport lodged at GWENT Fm. Lt MITTERBURGER & entered 6707 F.A. 3 Subsections M.T.W attached 31 M.A.C.	
	18/XI/17		Pte CARTER 63969 + Pte CHADWICK 63852 were killed by shell fire this morning at Regt. Aid Post. Major McAFEE, Lieut PEACE & 180.O.R. returned from 46 C.C.S. today for duty	
	19/XI/17		27144 Cpl HANDY W.B. posted Ltein[?] with him were in place of Cpl GERATY evacuated wounded. Capt McAFEE proceeded to A.D.S. MINTY FARM in relief	
	20/XI/17		of Capt INNES who returned to ESSEX FARM.	

WAR DIARY or INTELLIGENCE SUMMARY

Army Form C. 2118

Place	Date	Hour	Summary of Events and Information	Remarks and references to Appendices
ESSEX FARM	21/XI/17		Lieut ARNOLD V.S.R. rejoined unit from A.D.S. MINTY. F.M. Trench foot prevention hut at KEMPTON PARK inspected.	
	22/XI/17		Nothing to report.	
	23/XI/17		A.D.S. St JULIAN & MINTY visited this morning.	
	24/XI/17		A.D.S. at St Julien & Minty visited by A.D.M.S., also trench foot treatment hut at KEMPTON PARK. 107 F.A. beaver divn relieved bearers of JP	
	25/XI/17		106 F.A. in St Julien sector. Capt HERATY returned at A.D.S. St Julien. Officer at VENHEULE A.D.S. withdrawn	SP
	26/XI/17		Lieut MOONEY. V.S.R. with drawn from A.D.S St Julien. Two officers nuo at SP St Julien Flem & at VENHEULE	
	27/XI/17		106 F.A. Beaver Divn relieved 105 F.A. bearers in line at MINTY. 63367 ⁰/ Cpl KNIGHT evacuated wounded.	SP
	28/XI/17		Lieut PENCE V.S.R. proceeded to temp. duty as M.O. 2/ RHLI.	SP
	29/XI/17		A.D.S. visited. Pte MORDECAI M2/50173 wounded today.	SP
	30/XI/17		O.C. 11 M.A.C. visited A.D.S. here. Found water mains in order today.	

Confidential.

Vol 23

War Diary

of

105th FIELD AMBULANCE. R.A.M.C.

From

1st December 1917.

to

31st December 1917.

Inclusive.

Volume XXIII.

Original.

COMMITTEE FOR THE MEDICAL HISTORY OF THE WAR
Date —1 FEB. 1918

Army Form C. 2118.

WAR DIARY
or
INTELLIGENCE SUMMARY.
(Erase heading not required.)

Place	Date	Hour	Summary of Events and Information	Remarks and references to Appendices
ESSEX FARM	1/xii/17		H.Q. of ambulance at ESSEX Fm. Evacuating cases from Divisional front from about M14 a 6.8 to v.25.a.6.1. Sept 20 A.D.S.'s at MINTY Farm, St JULIAN	
			Bearers of 3 F.A.'s pooled under O.C. 105 F.A. used in turn for evacuating from R.A.P's to A.D.S.	
	2/xii/17		L.t. E.B. PEACE returned from temp. charge of 18 H.L. A.D.S.'s visited	
	3/xii/17		Most well at MINTY	
	4/xii/17		Nothing to note	
			Sgt ANDERSON T.S. 4771, L-Cpl TAAFE T.63872, & Pte BROWN 63901 were this day presented with ribands of military medal by G.O.C. II Corps	
	5/xii/17		Medical Personnel preparing to transfer of unclassifying P.B. personnel of the 125 F.A. Zone of Division extending northwards & A.D.S. at CEMENT HOUSE Taken over from 53rd F.A. V.28.c.2.2.	

Army Form C. 2118.

WAR DIARY
or
INTELLIGENCE SUMMARY.

(Erase heading not required.)

Place	Date	Hour	Summary of Events and Information	Remarks and references to Appendices
ESSEX FARM	3/9/17		Ambulance cars of 356 been in previously attached to No 11 M.A.C. left here by Fr Kent & Evacuation for the time M.D.S. & C.M.D.S. Cement rest by this unit.	
	6/9/17		Nil, to note.	
	7/9/17		74286 Pt HICKMAN evacuated sick on 3rd Sept & struck off the strength of 75th.	
	8/9/17		M.D.S. at MINTY, ST JULIEN & CEMENT HOUSE returned to HOME COUNTIES F.A. attached personnel of 106 & 107 F.A. returned to their units.	
HERZEELE	9/9/17		Ambulance proceeded to HERZEELE & took over the 77th Cas. Rest Station from 107 & F.A. LIEUT E.A. CHRISTOFFERSEN M.O.R.C. U.S.A. proceeded to 106 F.A. for Temporary duty.	
	10/9/17		Nothing to note.	
	11/9/17		LIEUT E.B. PEACE M.O.R.C. U.S.A. & 3 O.R. proceeded to II rd Corps Schools Camp for Temporary duty.	

Army Form C. 2118.

WAR DIARY
or
INTELLIGENCE SUMMARY.
(Erase heading not required.)

Instructions regarding War Diaries and Intelligence Summaries are contained in F. S. Regs., Part II. and the Staff Manual respectively. Title pages will be prepared in manuscript.

Place	Date	Hour	Summary of Events and Information	Remarks and references to Appendices
HERZEELE	19/12/17		LIEUT C.H. ARNOLD M.O.R.C. U.S.A. proceeded to Embarcy duty L. of C. London	
	28/12/17		LIEUT E.A. CHRISTOFFERSEN rejoined the Unit.	
	14/12/17		No. 43585 Pte BALL W. rejoined to 24 South Midland F.A. Nothing to report	
	15/12/17		No. 29669 Pte FOSTER A.D. evacuated sick. Nothing to report	
	16/12/17		"	
	17/12/17			
	18/12/17			
	19/12/17		No. 56084 Pte RIDYARD, J. A.S.C. M.T. & Taken on the Strength, R.7.65	
Dunkirk to 4th Army	20/12/17		Unit.	
	21/12/17		Nothing to report	
	22/12/17		Capt E. PHILLIPS M.C. proceeded on leave to ENGLAND	
	23/12/17		T/Capt D.J. McAFEE awarded Military Cross.	
	24/12/17		Nothing to report	
	25/12/17			
	26/12/17		Capt D.J. McAFEE proceeded a leave to England. 1 Cpl PERRY W.A. one 1 Pte W. No 2 Aux Bos Coy M.S.C. Taken on Strength under authority ADMS 52.Div...E.Cavy/254/A.D.S.	

Army Form C. 2118.

WAR DIARY
or
INTELLIGENCE SUMMARY.
(Erase heading not required.)

Place	Date	Hour	Summary of Events and Information	Remarks and references to Appendices
HERZEELE	27/11/17		63657 Pte HODGINS promoted to A/Cpl. Confirmed with A.ng A. 27/11/17	
	28/11/17			
	29/11/17		Nothing to report.	
	30/11/17			
	31/12/17		Div. Motor Ambulances detailed to collect sick slowly from 157 & 159th Brigades & S.A.C	J. Duffield Lieut. O.C. 125 F.A.

CONFIDENTIAL.

WAR DIARY.

— OF —

105th. FIELD AMBULANCE. R.A.M.C.

— FROM —

1st. JANUARY 1918.

— TO —

31st. JANUARY 1918.

INCLUSIVE.

VOLUME XXIV.   ORIGINAL.

Army Form C. 2118.

WAR DIARY
or
INTELLIGENCE SUMMARY.
(Erase heading not required.)

Place	Date	Hour	Summary of Events and Information	Remarks and references to Appendices
HERZEELE Sheet 20 D 9 d 9.7	1/I/18		Ambulance at Chateau running 35th D.R.S.	
			1 M.O. detached temp duty I/c 14th Gloster Regt.	
			2 M.O.'s on leave to England	
			1 M.O. detached I/c reinforcement camp HOUTKERQUE	PP
			Unit but at rest, leaves being granted daily from	PP
	2/I/18		Lieut. C.H. ARNOLD R.S.R. returned from temp duty I/c 14 Gloster Regt.	PP
	3/I/18		Training of unit carried out. H.T. inspected	
	4/I/18		Mutiny troth.	PP
			The M.G.C. b'in dirs inspected the H.T. of this unit with that of	
			the other ambulances of the div'n at HOUTKERQUE this morning	PP
	5/I/18		Capt. E. PHILLIPS R.A.M.C. rejoined from 14 days leave (England)	
	6/I/18			
CANADA FM	7/I/18		Unit moved to CANADA FARM + relieved 2/3 H.C. F.A. (two Divisions)	
Sheet 28 A.18 a 2.7			personnel proceeded by train to ELVERDINGHE. Transport by road	
			D.R.S. opened at CANADA FM. 2/3 H.C. F.A. relieved this	
			unit at HERZEELE	
			Capt. J.W. INNES R.A.M.C. detached for temp'y duty c 106 FA.	PP

Army Form C. 2118.

WAR DIARY
or
INTELLIGENCE SUMMARY.
(Erase heading not required.)

Instructions regarding War Diaries and Intelligence Summaries are contained in F. S. Regs., Part II. and the Staff Manual respectively. Title pages will be prepared in manuscript.

Place	Date	Hour	Summary of Events and Information	Remarks and references to Appendices
CANADA FARM	8/1/17		Two ears with drivers rodster proceeded to 106 F.A. for duty.	
	9/5/17		Capt HEGATY R.A.M.C. proceeded on 14 days leave to England	DP
			Lt=Col. SCAIFE R.A.M.C " " " " "	SP
			72 teams & 5 N.C.O's proceeded to 106 F.A. for temp duty	SP
			Stables caught fire & horses destroyed. One half of stables + O.S.C hut destroyed	DP
	10/5/17		R.D.M.S. visited inspected hospital + site of fire.	SP
	11/5/17		87194 Pte BROMLEY proceeded to attend a course of cooking at 4th Army School of Cookery HAZEBROUCK	SP
	12/5/17		D.D.M.S. visited + inspected Hospital arranges to open C.R.S. so that O.C. evacuation could be relieved	SP
	13/5/17		Inquiry by Div. Claim officer to fire.	
	14/5/17		R.D.M.S. visited + inspected one of trench fort in hospital	SP
	15/5/17		History taken	—
	16/5/18		Lieut CHRISTOFFERSON S.A. M.O.R.C. U.S.A. proceeded to temp duty to 106 F.A.	SP

WAR DIARY
or
INTELLIGENCE SUMMARY.

(Erase heading not required.)

Army Form C. 2118.

Place	Date	Hour	Summary of Events and Information	Remarks and references to Appendices
CANADA FARM				
	17/1/18		Lieut C.A. ARNOLD M.C. U.S.R. proceeded on leave to PARIS	
	18/1/18		Capt INNES J.W. R.A.M.C. rejoined unit from 106 F.A.	
	19/1/18		D.D.M.S. inspected cart. 10023 Pte HODGE T. R.A.M.C. evacuated to 46 C.C.S.	
	20/1/18		Pte TRAINER T. 2646 posted to this unit from 2 C.C.S.	
	21/1/18		Nothing to report	
	22/1/18		Work continued on horse stall, Roads, Repairing of stables in camp	
	23/1/18		204142 Pte LENNARD R. 5th K.S.L.I. posted to this unit taken on the strength. 1	
	24/1/18	10.0am	Court of Inquiry in the fire at the stables on 9th inst. Capt. T. KEATY R.A.M.C. rejoined unit from leave to ENGLAND Capt. C.A. ARNOLD M.C. U.S.R. rejoined unit from leave to PARIS	
	25/1/18		Lieut C.H. ARNOLD never Manuel letter rank of Capt. (Actg. Mason Officer. Admiral Home E.C.4 dtd 14/1/18) Lt-Col SCAIFE ?? rejoined unit from leave to ENGLAND	

Army Form C. 2118.

WAR DIARY
or
INTELLIGENCE SUMMARY.
(Erase heading not required.)

Instructions regarding War Diaries and Intelligence Summaries are contained in F. S. Regs., Part II. and the Staff Manual respectively. Title pages will be prepared in manuscript.

Place	Date	Hour	Summary of Events and Information	Remarks and references to Appendices
CAMABATIN.	26/1/18		A.D.M.S. visited the Special Hospital. Orders received for Capt HEGARTY	
			R.A.M.C. – Lieut CHRISTOFFERSON to proceed on 29th to units	AP
	27/1/18		between Kenfant	AP
	28/1/18		" " "	AP
	29/1/18		Capt ARNOLD C.H. M.C.R.R proceeded to 106 F.A. for duty in relief of Lieut.	AP
			E.A. CHRISTOFFERSON M.C.U.S.R. who proceeded for duty as M.D.!c 23rd Munsheeben	
			Capt T.F. HEGARTY R.O.M.S. proceeded for duty as MO/c 35 D.J.R.G	
	30/1/18		M.O.M.S. inspected the hospital at Camp.	AP
	31/1/18		history kept.	AP

[signature]
Lu Col. 10 S.P.A.

CONFIDENTIAL.

WAR DIARY

— OF —

105th. FIELD AMBULANCE. R.A.M.C.

FROM

1st. FEBRUARY 1918.

— to —

28th. FEBRUARY 1918.

INCLUSIVE.

VOLUME XXV.   ORIGINAL.

WAR DIARY
or
INTELLIGENCE SUMMARY.
(Erase heading not required.)

Army Form C. 2118.

Place	Date	Hour	Summary of Events and Information	Remarks and references to Appendices
CANADA FARM. Sheet 28 A 18 a 9.7	1/2/18		Much rain here running a BS in 300-400 patients, 295 patients at present in Brown detached into 10b BA Evacuation in casualties from front line.	
	2/2/18		Medical Board assembled today in T/2/Lt RODDA DHLW R.S.C. with continued in rebuilding of stables resulting of huts, averaging of yarton + general repairs. Total patients ring 277	
	3/2/18		Patients ring 264	
	4/2/18		Patients ring 253	
	5/2/18		1 WO, 1 NCO + 5 men R.S.C proceeded to QQMS to draw remounts Patients ring 225	
	6/2/18		Lt. L.A.H. BULKLEY R.A.M.C posted to this unit from M.O i/c 155 Chinkwhito. Patients ring 248	
	7/2/18		Unit continued in camp, rebuilding of huts, stables + general repairs. Patients ring 253	
	8/2/18		Lieut L.A.H BULKLEY RAMC proceeded for temporary duty as	

WAR DIARY
or
INTELLIGENCE SUMMARY.
(Erase heading not required.)

Army Form C. 2118.

Place	Date	Hour	Summary of Events and Information	Remarks and references to Appendices
	8/2/18		M.O. ½ 15g Bde RFA	
			No 27144 Cpl HANDY W.B. R.A.M.C. reverted to ranks (Auth II Cps "A" D.F./1991 dated 1/2/18) Posted to duty c̄ 106 F.A.	B/1
			Bearers attached 106 F.A. rejoined their today	
			4 O.R reinforcements arrived here to duty.	
			Patients msg 265	
	9/2/18		Lt. R.J. HELSBY R.A.M.C. (Temp) posted letter went from M.O. ½c	B/1
			24. L. F.	
			1 O.R. posted to their unit today. Patients msg 266.	
	10/2/18.		2 O.R. posted to their unit today. 1 O.R. evacuated sick.	B/1
			Patients msg 267	
	11/2/18		4 NCOs & 51 bearers proceeded to 107 F.A. for duty today	B/1
			Patients msg 290	
	12/2/18.		1 O.R. evacuated sick struck off strength	B/1
			Patients msg 298	
	13/2/18		1 O.R posted letter went Patients msg 299.	B/1

Army Form C. 2118.

WAR DIARY
or
INTELLIGENCE SUMMARY.
(Erase heading not required.)

Instructions regarding War Diaries and Intelligence Summaries are contained in F. S. Regs., Part II. and the Staff Manual respectively. Title pages will be prepared in manuscript.

Place	Date	Hour	Summary of Events and Information	Remarks and references to Appendices
CANADA	14/3/18		Work continued in reviewing of huts, disinfecting while waiting. Patients nuy 297	
	15/3/18		Patients nuy 294	
	16/3/18		I.O.R. held Intin unit. Patients nuy 286	
	17/3/18		I.O.R. inspected sick. Patients nuy 286	
	18/3/18		Lieut HELSBY R.I. R.A.M.C. proceeded from temporary duty in M.O'/c 15 Sherwoods	
		Wesh.	Col CHISE HOORE C.M.G. D.D.M.S. I st Corps inspected us unit and general arrangements. Patients nuy 273.	
	19/3/18		Col MIDDLETON D.S.O. A.D.D.S. 35 Div. made careful inspection of latrine unit, camp flushing. Patients nuy 272	
	20/3/18		Work continued on camp dwellings. Our faces have now been cleaned up. Patients nuy 252	

WAR DIARY
or
INTELLIGENCE SUMMARY.
(Erase heading not required.)

Army Form C. 2118.

Place	Date	Hour	Summary of Events and Information	Remarks and references to Appendices
OMAPA FARM	21/7/18		Patients Heavy more treatment 281	"
	22/7/18		" " " 274	"
	23/7/18		Capt C.H. ARNOLD MCUSR proceeded on leave to UK	"
			1 OR hiked to train unit	"
			Patients avg 278	"
	24/7/18		" " 272	"
	25/7/18		Lieut L.H. BULKLEY RAMC rejoined unit from 159 Bde R=A	"
	26/7/18		Revetting of huts almost completed. Huts in garden continued	"
	27/7/18		Lt LPA BULKLEY RAMC & 1 N.C.O. proceeded today to Fourth Army RAMC School	"
			1 O.R. evacuated wounded	
			Patients avg 274	
	28/7/18		Nothing to report. Patient avg 270.	"

P. Mun
Capt RAMC
to O.C. 105 F.A.

CONFIDENTIAL.

WAR DIARY

OF

105th. FIELD AMBULANCE

R.A.M.C.

FROM

1st. MARCH 1918.

TO

31st. MARCH 1918.

INCLUSIVE

COMMITTEE FOR THE MEDICAL HISTORY OF THE WAR
Date 12 MAY 1918

VOLUME XXVI.   ORIGINAL.

Army Form C. 2118.

WAR DIARY
or
INTELLIGENCE SUMMARY.
(Erase heading not required.)

Instructions regarding War Diaries and Intelligence Summaries are contained in F. S. Regs., Part II. and the Staff Manual respectively. Title pages will be prepared in manuscript.

Place	Date	Hour	Summary of Events and Information	Remarks and references to Appendices
CANADA FARM Sheet 28 A.18.A.2.7	1/11/18		R. Unit established here running as D.R.Stn accomodation 350 patients	
			2 Recurs detached for duty c̄ 107 F.A.	
			Patients in hospital 284	SP
	2/11/18		Unit being revetted, stables repaired, agriculture being energetically dealt with	
			Patients in hospital 289	SP
	3/11/18		Six reinforcements posted Lilly with today. Patients in hospital 296	SP
			The NCO proceeded treated the 2nd Cps anti gas school	
	4/11/18		Capt J W INNES R.A.M.C. proceeded to temporary duties as M.O. 11e 15th Devon's	SP
			Lt R.T. HELSBY R.A.M.C. rejoined this unit fm 15th Devon's	
	5/11/18		" " " posted to 159 Bde R.F.A. as M.O. Stuart's	SP
			of the strength of this unit	
	6/11/18		Normal routine work continued. Patients in hospital 281	SP
	7/11/18		" " " " 301	SP
	8/11/18		Capt J W INNES R.A.M.C. returned fm 15th Devon's	SP
			2 men evacuated gassed, 2 sick.	SP

Army Form C. 2118.

WAR DIARY
or
INTELLIGENCE SUMMARY.
(Erase heading not required.)

Place	Date	Hour	Summary of Events and Information	Remarks and references to Appendices
CANADA FARM	9/14/18		Usual routine hospital work carried on. Patients in hospital 291	AP
	10/14/18		Capt S.A. BULL RAMC noted little work for duty, taken in strength.	
			Reserve attached to 107 FA reports this unit today	AP
	11/14/18		Usual routine hospital work carried on. Patients in hospital 236	AP
	12/14/18		Lieut L.A.H BULKELEY RAMC proceeded for Tempy duty with 1/9 D.L.I	AP
	13/14/18		Lieut E.B. PEACE MC VSR transferred as MO to 5g. Bde RGA. T struck off strength	AP
	14		1 N.C.O proceeded to attend the 2nd course of Fourth Army RAMC Oct. 18	AP
	14/14/18		Whole unit inspected this day by ADMS 35 Div	AP
	15/14/18		Nothing to report. Patients in hospital 187	AP
	16/14/18		Capt C.H. ARNOLD, MC US.R. proceeded for temp duty with 5g. Bde RGA. Capt E PHILLIPS & Capt J.W. INNES RAMC are given authority, travel, baggage of Majors 35 Div A. 11/83. 01.15.7/18	AP
	17/14/18		ADMS 35 Div inspected the whole unit at 8.30 hr Useful March over	AP
			5 reinforcements posted to this unit for duty	AP

WAR DIARY or INTELLIGENCE SUMMARY

Army Form C. 2118.

Place	Date	Hour	Summary of Events and Information	Remarks and references to Appendices
CANADA FARM.	18/III/18		Capt. JAMES R.A.M.C. from No 11 C.C.S. is posted to this unit (he is at present on leave) to take over his charge.	
	19/III/18		Usual routine work carried on. Patients admitted 146	
	20/III/18		" " " " "	
	21/III/18		" " " " "	
	22/III/18		Capt. M. BULL R.A.M.C. transferred as R.M.O. 17th b.F.A. whole strength of WHITING attached to this unit to return but not taken in his strength	
	23/III/18		105 F.A. personnel transferred, arrived at PESEL HOEK 4.0.p.m. today to CORBIE. C.O. & M.C. (M.T) personnel & motor ambulance cars (5 weeks) by road to CORBIE. All patients & kit handed over to No 2 F.A. 1st D.V.	
	24/III/18		train arrived CORBIE about 10 a.m. after detraining unit proceeded w/c Major J.W. INNES by road to CERISY Sheet 62D Q8 c central arriving there at 4.30 p.m. been received from H.Q.A.D.S. for 110 hours, 5 N.C.O. & others to join 106 F.A. at 8 ETINHEM. Under instruction from H.Q.R. & Rest D.20,C,5/106.29. only	

WAR DIARY
or
INTELLIGENCE SUMMARY.
(Erase heading not required.)

Army Form C. 2118.

Place	Date	Hour	Summary of Events and Information	Remarks and references to Appendices
CERISY 62.Q8c	24/III/18	⊙	50 bearers & 3 N.C.O's were sent remainder held in readiness here	A/P
			AM. Unit except men borage me detached from early c 106 F.A.	A/P
	25/III/18		Unit as above remains here. Orders received at 11.50 am to move forward to SAILLY-Le-Sec	A/P
SAILLY-Le-SEC 62 J28d	26/III/18	7am	Ambulance arrived here & was billeted for the night	A/P
			Orders received to proceed forthwith via BOIRE to LAVIEVILLE. On arrival there, the unit was instructed to proceed to HENENCOURT	
		2pm	Ambulance bivouaced at HENENCOURT, Capt McAFEE & bearers rejoined Unit. They moved under instruction from 3rd Brit'h Q. The ambulance moved to WARLOY	
		6pm	Ambulance established at WARLOY	
WARLOY 27/III/18			2 N.C.O's + 28 men with wheeled stretchers attached as bearers to 107 H.A.	A/P
BAILLON AMIENS 1/10000 Q6,3	28/III/18		Main Dressing Sta opened here	A/P
	29/III/18		M.D.S. remained in relief	A/P
	30/III/18		Bearers returned from 107 P.A.	A/P
LAHOUSSAYE 62 B18.9.9	31/III/18		Ordered to proceed to LAHOUSSAYE tomorrow	
			Unit arrived here 11.50 am. Sick collected from 105 Bde.	

William Magin Rome Lt
A.O.C 105 Fd.

A.5.3 Wt. W11422/M160 350,000 12/16 D.D.&L. Forms/C./2118/4.

CONFIDENTIAL.

WAR DIARY

— OF —

105th. FIELD AMBULANCE

R.A.M.C.

— FROM —

1st. APRIL 1918.

— TO —

30th. APRIL 1918.

INCLUSIVE

VOLUME XXVII.   ORIGINAL.

WAR DIARY
or
INTELLIGENCE SUMMARY.

Army Form C. 2118.

Place	Date	Hour	Summary of Events and Information	Remarks and references to Appendices
LAHOUSSOYE	1/iv/18		Unit resting here in billets/tents. Sick being evacuated from 104 F.A. to evacuated T.106 F.A in this village	
	2/iv/18		Capt. ARNOLD C.H. M.C. U.S.R. returned from Temp. duty M.O. 53 Bn. F.A.	
	3/iv/18		Capt. ARNOLD C.H. proceeded to duty c. 18 L.F. Capt. CHARTERS F.A.M.C. (to) posted Lieutenant Capt. BUCKLEY F.A.M. R.M.C. (to) a relief from 19 F.S.I. Arrived 1st S. Churches Church St Surrgts Capt INNES R.A.M.C. [held] To 106 F.A. & " "	
	4/iv/18		Lt E.W. STONE M.O.V.R. posted to this unit with LT. McAFEE	
	5/iv/18		Unit temporarily attached to 5 Australian Divn. cars included etc &	
			craned totter	
TOUTENCOURT	6/iv/18 7/iv/18	am	Unit moved to TOUTENCOURT arriving 7.30 p.m. Unit remained here under rest/line training	
VARENNES	8/iv/18		Unit moved to VARENNES + took over evacuation of sick + wounded of Bn. Ain Amt A.55 at HEDAUVILLE with R.A.P.s near BOUZINCOURT +	

A6945 Wt. W14422/M1160 350,000 12/16 D.D. & L. Forms/C./2118/14.

WAR DIARY
or
INTELLIGENCE SUMMARY.

(Erase heading not required.)

Army Form C. 2118.

Instructions regarding War Diaries and Intelligence Summaries are contained in F. S. Regs., Part II. and the Staff Manual respectively. Title pages will be prepared in manuscript.

Place	Date	Hour	Summary of Events and Information	Remarks and references to Appendices
			MARTINSART. Our first breakfast at ENGLEBELMER. Crosses erected to	PP
VARENNES	9/10/18		V Corps at MARTINSART	
			Relief completed and all units taken over from 4 & 5 divns TAS	PP
			47 bgn by 9.0 am	
			Parties of bearers sent from 106 & 107 FA attached fifteen	PP
			with for duty. Capts V.N.B. WILLIS + L.P. BRENT RAMC	PP
			posted within week.	
			Personnel attached T CWOCP + CWODS to temping duty.	PP
			BoR attached 105-Rcd H.Q. 4/c foot-bullies.	
	10/11/18		Capt CHARTERIS at ADS relieved by Capt BRENT	PP
			Capt LUTHERLAND came posted tothin unit.	
	11/11/18		Two stretchers attached from 106 FA. Intern unit. Beaurevoir	PP
			105 FA relieved is lieu by 106 FA	
	12/11/18		Capts G.E. CHARTERS RAMC proceeded to Ent. to 17 RGT.	
			Pte BARNET, BARTLEMAN, McDADE, Sgt CAMPBELL awarded Military Medal	PP
	13/11/18		ENGLEBELMER Cov. hot destroyed by shell fire + four casualties.	PP

WAR DIARY
or
INTELLIGENCE SUMMARY.
(Erase heading not required.)

Army Form C. 2118.

Place	Date	Hour	Summary of Events and Information	Remarks and references to Appendices
VRENNES	13/IV/18		Weather deteriorated everyday. 3 OR gassed at	JP
	14/IV/18		SICK 4/3	
			Capt V.N.B. WILLIS RAMC proceeded to A.D.S. in relief of Lt DAVIES	JP
	14/IV/18		Men's also returned here	
	15/IV/18		Bearers of 106 M. relieved in line by men of 107 M.	JP
	16/IV/18		Capt T.W. SUTHERLAND CAMC returned to N°8 C. Sta. Hospital	JP
	17/IV/18		Nothing unusual	JP
	18/IV/18		Nothing to report	JP
	19/IV/18		Bearers of 107 M. relieved by those of 105. M.	JP
			Sgt GUERIN 63856 awarded military medal	JP
	20/IV/18		1 O.R. killed by shellfire at ENGLEBELMER	JP
	21/IV/18		Capt WILLIS RAMC returned to HQ from ADS in relief to	JP
			Lieut STONE MC U.S.R. to waits proceeded to the field Railway	
	22/IV/18		Nothing unusual	JP
	23/IV/18		Bearers of 105 M. relieved by bearers of 106 M.	
			Capt WILLIS proceeded to A.D.S. via 19 D.L.I in relief of Capt DAVIES	JP

WAR DIARY
or
INTELLIGENCE SUMMARY.
(Erase heading not required.)

Army Form C. 2118.

Place	Date	Hour	Summary of Events and Information	Remarks and references to Appendices
	25/iv/18		Major Ico Joines relieved Major Phillips at A.D.S. McDonville	
VARENNES			Captain N.B. Willis R.A.M.C. rejoined the unit from S.L.I.	
	26/iv/18		B.O.R. proceeded to 105 F.A. H.Q. for denial at Batery	
	27/iv/18		Bears of 106 M.A. relieved by bearers of 107 M.A.	
	28/iv/18		holiday to refresh	
	29/iv/18		Capt. L.P. BESANT R.A.M.C. relieved by Lt. E. WALTON R.A.M.C. at A.D.S. McDAUVILLE	
	30/iv/18		Adm. returned from McDuil re-lading men to 38 D.D.	

[signature]
Major R.A.M.C.
i/c O.C. 105 F.A.

CONFIDENTIAL.

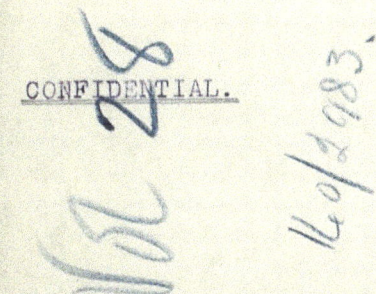

WAR DIARY

OF

105th. FIELD AMBULANCE
R.A.M.C.

FROM

1st. MAY 1918

TO

31st. MAY 1918

INCLUSIVE

VOLUME XXVIII.   ORIGINAL.

Army Form C. 2118.

WAR DIARY
or
INTELLIGENCE SUMMARY.
(Erase heading not required.)

Instructions regarding War Diaries and Intelligence Summaries are contained in F. S. Regs., Part II. and the Staff Manual respectively. Title pages will be prepared in manuscript.

Place	Date	Hour	Summary of Events and Information	Remarks and references to Appendices
VARENNES Sheet 57 P25d3.3	1/V/18		Evacuating casualties from line AVELUY WOOD & BOUZINCOURT. A.D.S. at HEDAUVILLE. Bearer posts at BOUZINCOURT & ENGLEBELMER.	
			Majr JAMES + 2 officers i/c A.D.S. HEDAUVILLE. Reserve bearers at VARENNES	✓P
			Bearers cars of 106 + 107 F. Ambs attached	
	2/V/18	9am	Bearer posts of R. subsectin handed over to 129 F.A. 38 Divn. A.D.S. HEDAUVILLE. Personnel from A.D.S.	
			" " " L " " " 131 " " "	
			" " " " " " " " " Attached personnel, cars &c of 106 + 107	
			Bearer subdivisions of unit returned.	
		2.0pm	Marched to HERISSART arriving 4.30pm. Accommodation for about 20	✓P
HERISSART T10.a.3.4.	3/V/18		patients arranged at Inschool. Hospital cleaned & arranged. Affairs re water	
			1 NCO & 10 men proceeded to Tincy 9 duty to 56 C.C.S.	✓P
	4/V/18		Capt G.M. GRANT R.A.M.C. (T.C) posted to this unit for duty	✓P
	5/V/18		bunk issued in entire Hospital + billet	✓P
	6/V/18		7 O.R. arrived from W.W.C.P. (36 F.A.)	✓P
			Practitioner by Capt Cecil of hr M rubbing tr 4 O.R. of their unit	✓P

WAR DIARY
or
INTELLIGENCE SUMMARY.

(Erase heading not required.)

Army Form C. 2118.

Instructions regarding War Diaries and Intelligence Summaries are contained in F. S. Regs., Part II. and the Staff Manual respectively. Title pages will be prepared in manuscript.

Place	Date	Hour	Summary of Events and Information	Remarks and references to Appendices
HERISSART	7/5/18		3 O.R. struck off strength in being evacuated to C.C.S.	MP
	8/5/18		Ambulances supplied with 105 Bde by Cps Commander.	
			Capt L.P. BRENT, A.A.M.C. proceeded from Temp duty a.M.O. 10/4 N.W.C. Staff	POP
	9/5/18		Usual routine work carried on. Bearers given technical training.	
	10/5/18		8 O.R. posted to this unit	
	11/5/18		holding trippete	
	12/5/18		Capt G.M GRANT RAMC, Capt V.N.B WILLIS AAMC & 12 O.R. proceeded to 3 C.C.S. for temp duty.	
	13/5/18		Nothing to report	
	19/5/18		Ambulance received to TOUTENCOURT taking over site from 106 F.A. & forming a DRS. New SP Vid 7.7.	
TOUTENCOURT			W.N.C.O.'s 60 Bearers & 2 Sunbeam Cars attached 106 FA	
"	20/5/18		Capt L.P. BRENT AAMC detailed to proceed daily to be sick at The right line.	
			M 109, 105, 106 Inf Bdes at HARPONVILLE	
	21/5/18		Bdes moved down to TALMAS in 3 sub Party proceeded there to arrange for	

Army Form C. 2118.

WAR DIARY
or
INTELLIGENCE SUMMARY.
(Erase heading not required.)

Instructions regarding War Diaries and Intelligence Summaries are contained in F. S. Regs., Part II. and the Staff Manual respectively. Title pages will be prepared in manuscript.

Place	Date	Hour	Summary of Events and Information	Remarks and references to Appendices
TOUTENCOURT	21/1/18		accumulation of patients	
"	22/1/18		Head qrs TALMAS opening at 10.30am. Patients transferred to TOUTENCOURT	
TALMAS			in M.A.C. cars. Bauso re made ready, received by patients.	
"	23/1/18		Work of receiving knows available for patients carried on with, existing	
			latrines, bath, ablution arrangements made	
			Capt L.B.BRENT A.A.M.C. proceeded to duty with 12 H.C.S. Much M. plus to	
"	24/1/18		Work carried on with camp.	
"	25/1/18		Lt E.W.STONE M.C.USR detached to take over Sanitary Medical charge 87-2s-Div.	
			Rec'd Increased wing TALMAS in relief of Capt WAINWRIGHT	
			Lt F.WALTON R.M.C proceeded for duty with 17th Royal Regt	
			Lt C.A.HILL 4/9835 proceeded to England under A.C.I. 1533/1917 on 24/14/65	
			in Church of England	
"	26/1/18		Work carried on with camp. D.D.M.S. IV Corps inspected the camp.	
"	28/1/18		Q.M.S.H. S/Sgt. HAY. A. mentioned in despatches L.G. 25/15/13	
"	29/1/18		D.M.S. Third Army is inspecting Lins. with tomorrow.	
			Total Beads (120) are being held here for 4 weeks for patients	

WAR DIARY
or
INTELLIGENCE SUMMARY.

(Erase heading not required.)

Army Form C. 2118.

Place	Date	Hour	Summary of Events and Information	Remarks and references to Appendices
TALMAS	30/4/18		D.D.M.S. visit cancelled this afternoon	RD
	31/4/18		Usual routine work carried on both covered in nursing	
			Number of men sick & bilious are rather reduced	(?)

Philip
Major R.A.M.C.
for O.C. 105TH FIELD AMBULANCE

CONFIDENTIAL.

WAR DIARY

OF

105th. FIELD AMBULANCE

R.A.M.C.

FROM

1st. JUNE 1918.

TO

30th. JUNE 1918.

INCLUSIVE.

VOLUME XXIX.   ORIGINAL.

WAR DIARY
or
INTELLIGENCE SUMMARY.
(Erase heading not required.)

Army Form C. 2118.

Place	Date	Hour	Summary of Events and Information	Remarks and references to Appendices
TROMM SP S3 D2.6	1/1/18		1. D.G. "Q" I/C Corps inspected the hospital this morning. Dufer Mess further taken in "Pas" this afternoon.	JP
	2.		Work carried on in D.R.S. exciting conditions ec.	JP
	3.		Q.M.S. SHRIMPTON 47613 & Sgt KEYWORTH 47005 approved britain's work.	JP
	4th.		Inflening Tréport	JP
	5th.		One O.R. evacuated wounded & one sick. D.D.M.S. V Corps visited the unit this afternoon	JP
	6th.		One O.R. died of wounds	JP
	7th.		Influing to front	JP
	8th.		D.D.M.S. V Corps visited buickfields unit today.	JP
	9th.		1 N.C.O. detailed to attend V Corps Gas School. 1 O.R. evacuated sick	JP
	10th, 11th, 12th		Usual routine work carried on	JP
	13.		Corps Commander & D.D.M.S., Divisional Commander with A.D.M.S. inspected the unit this afternoon.	JP
	14.		Work carried on as usual entripled ec.	JR

Army Form C. 2118.

WAR DIARY
or
INTELLIGENCE SUMMARY.
(Erase heading not required.)

Place	Date	Hour	Summary of Events and Information	Remarks and references to Appendices
TALMAS 57 b 53 d.6	16th		Work continued in Hospital premises. Bearers of trains which were attached to 107 FA. returned here today.	SB
	17th		1 OR transferred to 110 FA.	
	18th		2 OR of this unit awarded Meritorious Service Medals. "L.G." dated 18/6/18 2%	
	19th		1 OR evacuated sick T.C.S.	
	20th		D.D.M.S. visited unit and arranged site for Corps Rest in Depot. SB	
	21st		Lt D.I. VALENTINE MC RAMC (SR) joined this unit.	SB
			1 OR transferred to N°70 FA.	
	22nd		Capt G.M. GRANT RAMC returned from 3 CCS proceeded to 17th Royal Scots in relief of Lt WALTON RAMC, who proceeded to Aug F3 CCS.	SB
	23rd		Capt FREED transferred to this unit from 20 FA. & Taken on the strength.	SB
			Capt V.N.B. WILLIS RAMC evacuated sick to the Base.	SB
	24/		Usual routine work carried in leading trucks we started front carried on in "leading" enclosure	SB
	26th		1 OR admitted to this unit from SCCS	SB
	27/		D.A. and V Corps Mails arrived today	SB

Army Form C. 2118.

WAR DIARY
or
INTELLIGENCE SUMMARY.
(Erase heading not required.)

Instructions regarding War Diaries and Intelligence Summaries are contained in F. S. Regs., Part II. and the Staff Manual respectively. Title pages will be prepared in manuscript.

Place	Date	Hour	Summary of Events and Information	Remarks and references to Appendices
TOLMAS 57D S 3 d 2.6	28th		D.M.S. Third Army visited the unit today. Inspected hospital buildings etc.	
	29th		Personnel attached to 3 & 56 C.C.S. rejoined unit today.	
	30th		R&R evacuated pack to C.C.S. Awaiting orders to move at short notice.	
			Nita 104 1 See Appdx	

Phillips
Major R.A.M.C.
for O.C. No. 10 S.H.

A 60913 Wt. W14422/M1160 350,000 12/16 D. D. & L. Forms/C./2118/14.

CONFIDENTIAL.

WAR DIARY

OF

105th. FIELD AMBULANCE

R.A.M.C.

FROM

1st. JULY 1918

TO

31st. JULY 1918

INCLUSIVE

VOLUME XXX.   ORIGINAL.

WAR DIARY
or
INTELLIGENCE SUMMARY.
(Erase heading not required.)

Army Form C. 2118.

Place	Date	Hour	Summary of Events and Information	Remarks and references to Appendices
TALMAS 57D/40060 S.d.2.6	1/7/18		Unit marched to DOULLENS entraining there @ 1.30 PM under instructions issued by 104 I.Bde. Detrained St OMER 8PM & marched to St MARTIN/LAERT, arriving there 10.0pm & billeting in night. Ambulance cars proceeded by road from St M.	B
St MARTIN / LAERT	2nd		Personnel marched from TATINGHEM then proceeded by lorry to WATOU arriving at 11.30 pm billeting in the curved Abbee	B
			A.T. proceeded with 104 I.Bde transport leaving @ 4.0 pm but cars proceeded separately	B
WATOU 27D/40060 K4b5.5	3rd		Ambulance received the order, H.T. still with 104 I.Bde, 10% evacuated sick to Corps held colelcted from Bde. amb proceeded to cars	B
WATOU	3rd	1pm	Unit marched to TERDIGHEM where transport joined. Joined A.M.B. in place of French M.D.S.	B
TERDIGHEM Poog'1	5th		Received casualties the French and Belives 53 O.R. attached 107 M9 for lever julen	B
"	6th		Major J.W. HINES RAMC rejoined Unit 6/7/18 - 20/7/18	B

Army Form C. 2118.

WAR DIARY
or
INTELLIGENCE SUMMARY.
(Erase heading not required.)

Instructions regarding War Diaries and Intelligence Summaries are contained in F. S. Regs., Part II. and the Staff Manual respectively. Title pages will be prepared in manuscript.

Place	Date	Hour	Summary of Events and Information	Remarks and references to Appendices
FERDIGHEM	7th		Lieut F. WALTON RAMC proceeded for duty with 12 HCl.	AP
"	8th		Received at TERDINGHEM received orders to move out by 12 noon tomorrow to WATTEN BOESEGHEM	AP
WATTEN = BOESE = GHEM	9th		Arrived here at noon (midday) tent & opened as MDS	AP
	10th		Awaiting the French troops to evacuate, so that huts &c can be taken over	AP
	12		French troops evacuated today. Both Clearing + Walking wounded	AP
			arrangements made to receive [wounded?] which	
"	13		Lt VALENTINE RF, RAMC attached for temp duty into 157 Bde RFA	AP
"	14th		WO NCO attacked 4 N Staff in protection for one month with a view to commission in Infantry	AP
"			1 OR was to CCS struck off strength of Unit	AP
	15th		D.D.M.S. I Cps TRNS. 35 Div inspected the Unit	AP
			huts carried out this morning. Nothing even much to nothing to huts asked for for protection	

WAR DIARY
or
INTELLIGENCE SUMMARY.
(Erase heading not required.)

Army Form C. 2118.

Place	Date	Hour	Summary of Events and Information	Remarks and references to Appendices
TERDINGHEN	16/		Read 35 Div expected in end	
"	17th		Work carried on on round informing Buckeleding huts	
"	18th		Usual routine work continued	
"	20		D.M.S. seems Surrey Maj. Gen Ruggs-Moore DDMS & ADMS 35 Div visited The field Ambs this morning	
"	21		Usual routine work carried on	
"	22		Nothing to report	
"	23		Lt E.W. STONE proceeded to 17 L.F. for temp duty	
"	24th		Relieve of Capt LA BOUR who on return from leave will	
"			Usual routine work carried on though command	
"	25th		On returning home reported to MDS. Capt V.M.B. WILLIS RAMC, Corpl G.M. GRANT & Lt E. WILTON RAMC	
"	26th		posted to Induction troops off in charge of his units	
"			Nothing to report	
"	27th		Lt. J. T. FREEMAN (?) Noted keen went to duty	
"			Usual in his strength	

Army Form C. 2118

WAR DIARY
or
INTELLIGENCE SUMMARY
(Erase heading not required.)

Instructions regarding War Diaries and Intelligence Summaries are contained in F. S. Regs., Part II. and the Staff Manual respectively. Title Pages will be prepared in manuscript.

Place	Date	Hour	Summary of Events and Information	Remarks and references to Appendices
TER)INGHEM	28th		Usual routine work carried on. Road almost completed	
"	29th		Plinth erected for gun centre. Nothing to report	
"	30th		Lt D.J VALENTINE & me. Payne, proceeded to temporary duty (28 days) ½/c 4th N. Staff on relief of Lt W.G. HATS MP	
"	31st		Nothing to report	

P.P. Wigstiepen
Lieutenant
Engineer
in re -----

CONFIDENTIAL.

WAR DIARY.

OF

105th FIELD AMBULANCE.

FROM

1st AUGUST 1918.

TO

31st AUGUST 1918.

INCLUSIVE.

VOLUME XXXI.   ORIGINAL.

WAR DIARY or INTELLIGENCE SUMMARY

Army Form C. 2118

(Erase heading not required.)

Place	Date	Hour	Summary of Events and Information	Remarks and references to Appendices
ST SYLVESTRE CAPPEL SHEET 27 P.22.d.9.2.	29/9/18		Usual sick collected and work continued. J.W.J.	
	29/9/18	noon	105 Field Ambulance moved to Sheet 27. (Q.22.e.3.1.) 1 mile East of EECKE. taking over the Main Dressing Station from 110 Field Amb^{ce}, also the Advanced Dressing Station at LA ROSSIGNOL Sheet 27 (R.20.d.1.9.) and Bearer Posts. Relief completed by 12 noon. J.W.J.	
			Major D.J. VALENTINE R.A.M.C. (S.R.) and remaining personnel at QUEUE de VACHE rejoined the Unit. J.W.J.	
1 mile E. of EECKE	3/9/18	10.0 am	Main Dressing Station at 27/Q.22.e.3.1. taken over by 109 Field Ambulance 36th Divⁿ at 10.0 AM. J.W.J.	
ST SYLVESTRE CAPPEL			105 Field Amb^{ce} returned to ST SYLVESTRE CAPPEL again occupying the site at 27.P.22.d.9.2. J.W.J.	
			Advanced Dressing Station at LA ROSSIGNOL and Bearer Posts handed over to 109 Field Ambulance. Personnel rejoined H^{qrs} at ST SYLVESTRE CAPPEL arriving at 10.0 PM. J.W.J.	
			Sick collected from all Inf. Units of the Division. J.W.J.	

J.W. Jones
Major R.A.M.C.
for O.C. 105 Field Ambulance

Army Form C. 2118

WAR DIARY
or
INTELLIGENCE SUMMARY
(Erase heading not required.)

Instructions regarding War Diaries and Intelligence Summaries are contained in F. S. Regs., Part II. and the Staff Manual respectively. Title Pages will be prepared in manuscript.

Place	Date	Hour	Summary of Events and Information	Remarks and references to Appendices
ST SYLVESTRE CAPPEL SHEET 27 (P 22 d 9.2)	20/8/16		2 Sunbeam Cars attached to this Unit from 106 Field Amb'ce	J.W.J
	21/8/16		" " " " " 107 Field Amb'ce	J.W.J
			Lieut J.W. COPELAND. M.C.U.S.R. posted to this Unit and taken on the strength	J.W.J
			Usual sick collected and routine work carried on.	J.W.J
	22/8/16		2 Sunbeam Cars returned to 106 Field Amb'ce	J.W.J
			5 O.R.'s proceeded on leave.	J.W.J
	23/8/16		4 Sunbeam Cars returned to 107 Fd Amb'ce	J.W.J
	24/8/16		3 N.C.O's and 29 men transferred to Adv Dug Sta QUEUE de VACHE relieving a similar number	J.W.J
	25/8/16		One Ford Car attached to New Zealand Sanitary Section	J.W.J
			Usual sick collected and work carried on.	J.W.J
	26/8/16		2 O.R.'s proceeded on leave	J.W.J
	27/8/16		Ford Car returned from New Zealand Sanitary Section	J.W.J
	28/8/16		Lieut F. WALTON R.A.M.C. (S.R.) 1/1 N.C.O. acct. 16 men returned from Adv Dressing Station QUEUE de VACHE	J.W.J
			The following parties proceeded to the Adv Dug Sta LA ROSSIGNOL Shut 27 (R 20 d 7.7) prior to taking over from 110th Field Amb'ce
			Adv Dug Sta Pty:- Lieut R.W.B. GIBSON. S.A.M.C. Lieut E.W. STONE. M.C.U.S.R. Lieut F. WALTON R.A.M.C. 3 N.C.O's + 10 men	
			Bearer Party:- 3 N.C.O's and 148 Bearers.	J.W.J

WAR DIARY
or
INTELLIGENCE SUMMARY
(Erase heading not required.)

Army Form C. 2118

Place	Date	Hour	Summary of Events and Information	Remarks and references to Appendices
ST. SILVESTRE CAPPEL SHEET 27 (P22 d 9.2)	11/8/18		Lieut. J.T. HILL. R.A.M.C. (T.C.) transferred for duty with 12th Highland Light Inf. and struck off the strength. Usual sick collected.	J.W.9 J.W.9
"	12/8/18		"	J.W.9
"	13/8/18		Q.O.R's proceeded on leave. Sick collected from 104 Inf. Bde and 35th Div Artillery in addition to those previously stated.	J.W.9 J.W.9
"	14/8/18		Sick collected and routine work carried on. i.e. revaluation of horse lines etc. Training of personnel carried on.	J.W.9 J.W.9
"	15/8/18		"	J.W.9
"	16/8/18		42613 L/Cpl. S.A. SHRIMPTON. R.A.M.C. transferred to 96th Field Amb/ce and struck off the strength.	J.W.9
"	17/8/18		301025 S/Sgt W/Sgt GILLANDERS. J.F. R.A.M.C. (T) transferred to this Unit from 89th Field Amb/ce and taken on the strength. I.O.M. posted to this Unit. Usual sick collected.	J.W.9 J.W.9 J.W.9
"	18/8/18		Usual sick collected and routine work carried on.	J.W.9
"	19/8/18		8. O.R's proceeded on leave. Major R.W.B. GIBSON. R.A.M.C. (T) posted to this Unit and taken on the strength.	J.W.9 J.W.9
"	20/8/18		Lieut. F. WALTON. R.A.M.C. (S.R.) proceeded to Adv. Dsg Stn QUEUE de VACHE for duty.	J.W.9

WAR DIARY
INTELLIGENCE SUMMARY
(Erase heading not required.)

Army Form C. 2118

Place	Date	Hour	Summary of Events and Information	Remarks and references to Appendices
WAGENBRUGE SHEET 27 (P.10.d.2.3)	9/8/18	12 noon	Main Dressing Station at WAGENBRUGE handed over to 98th Field Amb. on 105 Field Amb. moved to ST SYLVESTRE CAPPEL taking over the camp vacated by 98th Field Amb. at (P.22.d.9.2) Sheet 27. Capt. D.F. VALENTINE. M.C. R.A.M.C. and Lieut J.T. HILL. R.A.M.C. and N.O. O.R.s proceeded to QUEUE de VACHE and took over the Dressing Station at (Q.11.d.2.6) Sheet 27 from 98th Field Amb.	J.W.J. J.W.J.
ST SYLVESTRE (CAPPEL) (SHEET 27 (P.22.d.9.2)	10/8/18		Sick collected from Units of 105 and 106 Inf. Bdes. All Bearer and Amb. Bars returned from 107 Field Amb. Sick collected as on the 9th inst. The following man awarded the MILITARY MEDAL by the G.O.C. Xth Corps for gallantry in action during recent operations. 67106 Pte. WARDEN. F.H. R.A.M.C. 29324 Pte. TRUSLOVE. L. R.A.M.C. 332208 Pte. BRAITHAUPT. G. R.A.M.C. The name of the following man has been brought to the notice of the higher Commander for gallantry displayed during a very heavy enemy bombardment on 4/8/18. Ve56.98. Pte. A. LINGARD. R.A.M.C.	J.W.J. J.W.J. J.W.J. J.W.J. J.W.J.
"	11/8/18		Lieut F. WALTON. R.A.M.C. (S.R.) posted to this Unit from 12th Highland Light Inf. and taken on the strength.	J.W.J.

WAR DIARY or INTELLIGENCE SUMMARY

Army Form C. 2118

(Erase heading not required.)

Place	Date	Hour	Summary of Events and Information	Remarks and references to Appendices
WAGENBRUGE SHEET 27 (P.12.d.2.3)	1/8/18		One O.R. evacuated sick and struck off strength.	f.w.d
"	2/8/18		Capt. D.J. VALENTINE. R.A.M.C. (S.R.) rejoined this Unit from H. of L Staff.	f.w.d
"	"		Major E. PHILLIPS. M.C. R.A.M.C. (R) having resumed command of 106 Field Ambulance, is struck off the strength of this Unit.	f.w.d
"	"		One O.R. transferred to 106 Field Ambulance and struck off strength.	f.w.d
"	"		3. N.C.O² and 130 Bearers attached to 107 Field Amb²⁾	f.w.d
"	"		Lieut COBB. M.C.U.S.R. attached to this Unit from 106 Field Amb⁾ for instruction.	f.w.d
"	3/8/18		Lieut E.W. STONE. M.C.U.S.R. rejoined this Unit from 17th Lancs Hus.	f.w.d
"	"		3 el.C.O² and 30 Bearers returned from 107 Field Amb⁾	f.w.d
"	4/8/18		8. O.R⁾ posted to this Unit.	f.w.d
"	5/8/18		3. N.C.O² and 30 Bearer attached to 107 Field Amb⁾	f.w.d
"	6/8/18		Nothing to report	f.w.d
"	7/8/18		" " "	f.w.d
"	8/8/18		" " "	f.w.d

CONFIDENTIAL.

WAR DIARY.

OF

105th FIELD AMBULANCE. R.A.M.C.

FROM

1st SEPTEMBER 1918.

TO

30th SEPTEMBER 1918.

INCLUSIVE.

VOLUME. XXXII.   ORIGINAL.

WAR DIARY
INTELLIGENCE SUMMARY
(Erase heading not required.)

Army Form C. 2118

Place	Date	Hour	Summary of Events and Information	Remarks and references to Appendices
MOORE	4/9/18		1 Other Rank proceeded on leave	J. W.J
PARK FARM	5/9/18		Nothing to report	
227 Ind Inf Bde	6/9/18		47098 Cpl. KEYWORTH. G. R.A.M.C. evacuated sick to N.Z. C.C.S. 2.8 6/9/18. J.W.J	
			87087 Pte. BUIN. H.G. R.A.M.C. died of wounds. 1 Other Rank evacuated wounded. J.W.J	
			70406 Pte. LYTH. J. R.A.M.C. proceeded to N° 2 Reinforcement Training Camp J.W.J	
			for transfer to 1st Bath South Wales Borderers. J.W.J	
			7 Other Ranks proceeded on leave.	
			Extract from List N° 203 of Appointments, Commands &c appeared	
			by the Field Marshall B.I.C. dated 1918.	
			"Lt. W/Lt Col Boring Major whilst commanding a section of a Field Amb."	
			Lieut D.J. VALENTINE (J.S.R.) 17th Aug 1918. J.W.J	
	7/9/18		One Other Rank evacuated sick.	J.W.J
	8/9/18		3 Other Ranks proceeded on leave.	J.W.J
			M/222942 Staff Sar/Mjr. G.L.HOOKER. A.S.C.(H.T.) proceeded to England for	J.W.J
			the purpose of taking a commission	J.W.J
	9/9/18		2 Other Ranks posted to this Unit	J.W.J
			" " (A.S.C. H.T.) evacuated sick.	J.W.J
	10/9/18		Nothing to report.	J.W.J
	11/9/18		1 Other Rank rejoined this Unit from 125 Inf Bde H.Q0. J.W.J	

WAR DIARY

INTELLIGENCE SUMMARY

Army Form C. 2118

Place	Date	Hour	Summary of Events and Information	Remarks and references to Appendices
ST SYLVESTRE CAPPEL (P.22.d.9.2)	1/9/18	9 A.M.	Lieut E. WALTON, R.A.M.C. and 11 Other Ranks returned to this Unit from QUEUE de VACHE. (27. Q.11.d.2.6.) 1 Other Rank attached to 105 Inf Bde HQrs to act as Orderly during the coming mov^t.	J.W.J.
"	2/9/18	2 P.M.	105 Field Ambulance moved with 105 Inf Bde, arriving at SCOUT CAMP (27/F.28.c.7.4.) at 2.0 P.M.	J.W.J.
SCOUT CAMP	"	6 P.M.	Major D.J. VALENTINE, M.C. R.A.M.C. and 2 N.C.O's proceeded to the Advanced Dressing Station, BELGIAN BATTERY CORNER. (28/H.24.a.5.8.) prior to taking over from 134 Field Ambulance. 8 Other Ranks proceeded on leave.	J.W.J.
"	3/9/18	5 P.M.	105 Field Amb^{ce} relieved N° 134 Field Amb^{ce} (30th American Divⁿ) Relief completed by 5-0 P.M. the following places being taken over: Field Amb^{ce} HQrs (27/G.4.d.4.4. White CHÂTEAU) VLAMERTINGHE. 28/H.8.2.7.8. Medical Aid Post at BRANDHOEK 28/G.12.4.6.6 HARBISON POST 28/G.3.2.5.5. and POPERINGHE 28/G.1.d.9.4.5. Adv. Dressing Sta. BELGIAN BATTERY CORNER 28/H.24.a.5.8. and Reserve Bearer Post. 28/I.19.d.2.5. Evacuation of lying cases by Mot^r Amb^{ce} and sitting cases by Lorry from WHITE CHÂTEAU VLAMERTINGHE to Divⁿ Walking Dressing Sta. BOWLBY CAMP. (27/E.6.d.central) 106 Field Amb^{ce}.	J.W.J.

WAR DIARY
or
INTELLIGENCE SUMMARY.
(Erase heading not required.)

Army Form C. 2118.

Place	Date	Hour	Summary of Events and Information	Remarks and references to Appendices
MOORE PARK FARM.	12/9/18		Under instructions from A.D.M.S. 35th Div: positions on left and right Bde. Sectors were recommended for the treatment of trench feet and the following places chosen. Left Bde. Sector 28/I.19.c.4.8. Right Bde. Sector 28/H.24.c.2.1. Other Ranks proceeded on leave.	J.w.f. J.w.f.
	13/9/18		Major J.W. INNES. R.A.M.C. assumed command of this Unit during the absence of Lieut-Col. B. Scarf R.A.M.C. on leave.	J.w.f.
	14/9/18		I.O.R. proceeded on leave. Lieut. G.W. STONE. M.O.R.C. took over command of Adv. Dressing Stn. relieving Major D.J. VALENTINE M.C. R.A.M.C. who turned to WHITE MILL.	J.w.f. J.w.f.
VLAMERTINGHE.	15/9/18		Capt. R.W.B. GIBSON. R.A.M.C. proceeded to White Mill. Vlamertinghe for duty. Major D.J. VALENTINE M.C. R.A.M.C. returned to Field Amb: H.Qrs.	J.w.f. J.w.f.
	16/9/18		Major D.J. VALENTINE M.C. R.A.M.C. proceeded to attend the 27th course at II Corps Anti-Gas School. MILLAIN.	J.w.f.
	"	12 noon	Divl. Main Dressing Station opened at White Mill. VLAMERTINGHE 28H.&9.3.	J.w.f.
HARBISON POST. 28/G.3.d.5.3. and Field Amb. Hdqrs at MOORE PARK FARM. 28/G.4.d.4.4. handed over to 14th Div. Field Amb. Hdqrs. moved to BRANDHOEK. 28/G.12.d.7.7.				J.w.f.

WAR DIARY or INTELLIGENCE SUMMARY.

Army Form C. 2118.

Place	Date	Hour	Summary of Events and Information	Remarks and references to Appendices
BRANDHOEK 28/9/12.5-9.7.	17/9/18		1 O.R. proceeded on leave. J.W.J. 2 O.R's attached to this Unit from 106 Fd. Amb's as a working party at Adv. Dressing Station 28th 4.24 a 6.8. J.W.J.	
	18/9/18		30 Bearers from 107 Field Amb's relieved Bearers of this Unit at Adv. Posts during night of 18th and 19th. J.W.J. 21 O.R's from 106 Field Amb's attached as working party at Adv. Post 28 I.19 d 8.5. J.W.J. 25 O.R's from 107 Fd. Amb't employed as working party at Adv Dressing Stat. J.W.J. 2 O.R's evacuated to C.C.S. and struck off the strength. J.W.J. Lieut. F. WALTON. R.A.M.C. returned to Whole Mill. VLAMERTINGHE from Adv. Dressing Sta. J.W.J.	
	19/9/18		Lieut. COBB. M.C. U.S.R. and A/Sgr. CHARLES. 106 Field Amb's proceeded to Advanced Dressing Station for instruction. J.W.J. Major D.J. VALENTINE. M.C. R.A.M.C. returned from 5 days leave under instructions from A.D.M.S. 35th Div and proceeded to Macor Dag. Sta. J.W.J.	
VLAMERTINGHE.			Lieut. F. WALTON. R.A.M.C. returned to Fd. Amb't. Hdqr BRANDHOEK. J.W.J.	

WAR DIARY or INTELLIGENCE SUMMARY

Army Form C. 2118.

Place	Date	Hour	Summary of Events and Information	Remarks and references to Appendices
BRAND HOEK 28/G.12.d.1.9	19/9/18		Capt. A.V. WEBSTER R.A.M.C. and 12 O.Rs. Ranks attached to this Fd. Amb. from No. 43. Fd. Amb. and remain at BRANDHOEK. J.W.T. Capt. A. SCOTT. R.A.M.C. and 13 Other Ranks attached to this Unit from No. 44 Field Amb. and employed at Main Dressing Sta. VLAMERTINGHE. J.W.T.	
	20/9/18		Arrangements made for the treatment of Trench Fever (n. SCHWAN. CHATEAU. J.W.T. 1 O.R. evacuated sick and struck off the strength. J.W.T.	
	21/9/18		2 O.R.'s A.&C. H.T. posted to this Unit. J.W.T.	
	22/9/18		Nothing to report. J.W.T.	
	23/9/18		Capt. A. SCOTT. R.A.M.C. and 13 O.R.'s returned to No. 44 Fd. Amb. J.W.T. 7 O.R.'s attached to this Unit from No. 43 Fd. Amb. J.W.T. The following Officers were attached to this Fd. Amb. in relief of Capt. A.V. WEBSTER. R.A.M.C. who returned No. 43 Fd. Amb. Capt. E.D. HAYES R.A.M.C. } 43 Field Ambulance Lieut. J.G. LOUDEN " J.W.T.	
	24/9/18	2 A.M.	The working party from 106 Fd. Amb. employed at Sud. Post 28/I.19.d.S.S. returned their Unit at 2.0 A.M. J.W.T. The working party from 106 Fd. Amb. employed at Adv. Dressing Sta. returned their Unit. J.W.T. Lieut. F. WALTON R.A.M.C. proceeded to Main Dressing Sta. VLAMERTINGHE. J.W.T.	

WAR DIARY
or
INTELLIGENCE SUMMARY.
(Erase heading not required.)

Army Form C. 2118.

Place	Date	Hour	Summary of Events and Information	Remarks and references to Appendices
BRANDHOEK 28/9 12£-17	24/9/18		Lieut COBB. M.C. V.S.R. returned 106 Field Amb.ce.	J.w.t.
	25/9/18		Lieut J. DEFNET. M.C. V.S.R. 106 Field Amb. proceeded to Adv. Dressing Sta.	J.w.t.
	26/9/18			
	27/9/18		N° 73/026513 Sgt. J. McCABE. A.S.C. (H.T) attached, awarded the Military Medal for gallantry and devotion to duty in action.	J.w.t.
			Major F. E. SPICER. R.A.M.C. 107 Fd. Amb. took charge of the Main Dressing Station.	J.w.t.
			WHITEMILL. VLAMERTINGHE returning Major D. J. VALENTINE. M.C. R.A.M.C. who returned to Fd. Amb. Hd.qrs.	J.w.t.
			Lieut J. DEFNET. M.C. V.S.R. returned to 106 Fd. Amb.ce	J.w.t.
			Lieut COBB. M.C. V.S.R. proceeded to Adv. Dressing Sta.	J.w.t.
			6 N.C.O.s and 72 Bearers proceeded up the line for duty under O.C. 106 Fd.Amb.	J.w.t.
			13 O.R.s proceeded on leave.	J.w.t.
	28/9/18		XIX th Corps Walking Wounded Station opened at BRANDHOEK	J.w.t.
		5-30am	At the commencement of the attack by this Divn, 105 Fd. Amb. was responsible for the Adv.Dressing Sta. 29/H.24 a.5.8. Main Dressing Sta, White Mill, VLAMERTINGHE 28/H.8 a.9.8. for Stretcher bearer and Corps Walking Wounded Sta. BRANDHOEK. 28/9.12.b.7.7.	J.w.t.

WAR DIARY or INTELLIGENCE SUMMARY

Army Form C. 2118.

Place	Date	Hour	Summary of Events and Information	Remarks and references to Appendices
BRANDHOEK	28/9/18		Medical Officers were distributed as follows :- Major J.W. INNES in command	
	12-1-7-7		XIV F.Amb. Walking Wounded Sta. Main Dug. Sta. Adv. Dug. Sta.	
			Major D.J. VALENTINE 1/c Major G.F. SPICER 1/c Lieut E.W. STONE	
			Capt. E.D. HAYES Capt. R.W.B. GIBSON Lieut COBB.	J. wt.
			Lieut J.G. LOUDEN Lieut F. WALTON	
			Lieut J.W. COPELAND	
			Number of cases passed through Main Dug. Sta. from 5-30 A.M. to 5-30 P.M. = 178 J. wt.	
			" " " " J. Corps Walking Wounded Sta. " " = 366 J. wt.	
	29/9/18		Major D.J. VALENTINE proceeded to Advanced Dressing Sta. relieving Lieut	
			E.W. STONE who returned to Fd. Amb. Major BRANDHOEK.	J. wt.
			Lieut F. WALTON and Lieut J.W. COPELAND proceeded to Adv. Dressing Sta.	J. wt.
			Lieut COBB returned to 106 Fd. Amt.	J. wt.
			Lieut Col. B. SCAIFE. R.A.M.C. returned from leave	J. wt.
			Major A.R. HILL. R.A.M.C. 106 Fd Amt returned from leave and	
			remained with this Unit at BRANDHOEK	J. wt.
			Lieut & D/y C.F. TYSON R.A.M.C. proceeded on leave	J. wt.
			Number of cases passed through Main Dug. Sta. from 5-30 P.M. 28/9/18 to 5-30 P.M. 29/9/18 91/K = 93 J. wt.	
			" " " " Corps W.W. Sta. " " = 337 J. wt.	

WAR DIARY
or
INTELLIGENCE SUMMARY.

Army Form C. 2118.

Place	Date	Hour	Summary of Events and Information	Remarks and references to Appendices
BRANDHOEK	29/9/18	7 P.M.	107 Field Ambulance took over the Main Dressing Sta. VLAMERTINGHE.	
	29 & 30.9.17		Lieut. E.W. STONE. M.C. U.S.R. proceeded on leave.	
			Number of cases passed through Main Dsg. Sta. from 5-30 P.M. 29/9/17 to 5-30 P.M. 30/9/17 = 161	
			" " " " " " " " " " " " " " Walking Wounded Sta. " = 395	

J. W. Turner.
Major. R.A.M.C.
for O.C. 106 Fd. Amb.

CONFIDENTIAL.

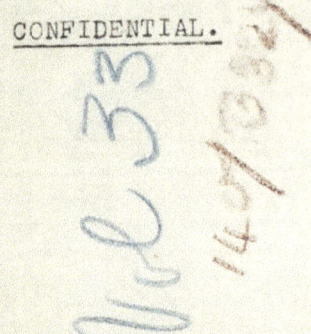

WAR DIARY.

OF

105th FIELD AMBULANCE. R.A.M.C.

FROM

1st OCTOBER 1918.

TO

31st OCTOBER 1918.

INCLUSIVE.

VOLUME. XXXIII.   ORIGINAL.

WAR DIARY
or
INTELLIGENCE SUMMARY.

Army Form C. 2118.

Place	Date	Hour	Summary of Events and Information	Remarks and references to Appendices
BRAND HOEK SHEET 28 G.12.6.7.7	1/10/18		Nothing to report	J.W.J.
	2/10/18		Capt. S. POTTER. R.A.M.C. (T.C.) posted to this Unit, and taken on the strength	J.W.J.
			Lieut F. WALTON. R.A.M.C. proceeded for temporary as M.O. of 157 Field R.F.A.	J.W.J.
			The following party returned to N° 3 Field Ambulance :-	J.W.J.
			Capt. E.D. HAYES R.A.M.C. Lieut J.G. LOUDEN. R.A.M.C. 18 Other Ranks. R.A.M.C.	J.W.J.
			The following party from 41st Div. Field Amb'ce were attached to this Unit for duty at the Baths Walking Wounded Sta.	
			Capt. F. P. WIGFIELD R.A.M.C. Lieut. J.W. ROBINSON. U.S.A.M.C. 17 Other Ranks. R.A.M.C.	J.W.J.
			Major A.R. HILL. R.A.M.C. returned to 106 Field Ambulance.	J.W.J.
			One O.R. evacuated wounded on 28/9/18.	J.W.J.
	3/10/18		Bearers returned to this Unit from 106 Field Ambulance.	J.W.J.
			One O.R. evacuated wounded.	J.W.J.
	4/10/18		Nothing to report.	J.W.J.
	5/10/18		" "	J.W.J.
	6/10/18		The personnel attached to this Unit from 41st Div¹ Field Ambulance on 2/10/18 returned to their Unit.	J.W.J.
			14 Other Ranks proceeded on leave.	J.W.J.
			Advanced Dressing Stig. BELGIAN BATTERY CORNER 28/H.29.a.3.8. taken over by 106 Field Ambulance.	J.W.J.

WAR DIARY or INTELLIGENCE SUMMARY

Army Form C. 2118.

Place	Date	Hour	Summary of Events and Information	Remarks and references to Appendices
BRANDHOEK 28/6.12.9.77	11/10/18		The following party proceeded for duty at the Combined Main Dressing Station of 1.30th field A.1.2st Regiment under O.C. 140th Field San 1st at the "ECOLE" YPRES. (Sheet 28 I 9 c.)	
			Capt. S. POTTER. R.A.M.C. Lt J.W. COPELAND. M.C. U.S.A. 22 Other Ranks. R.A.M.C.	J.W.J.
			1 N.C.O. and 2 men proceeded to White Mill VLAMERTINGHE as a billeting party	J.W.J.
			3 Bearer Squads (12 men) attached to 106 Fd Amb for duty	J.W.J.
			Capt. R.W.B. GIBSON. R.A.M.C. proceeded for temporary duty with 19th Inductian Depôt	J.W.J.
11/10/18			Nothing to report.	J.W.J.
12/10/18			" " "	J.W.J.
13/10/18			1 Other Rank. A.S.C. M.T. posted to this Unit.	J.W.J.
14/10/18			Major D.J. VALENTINE. M.C. R.A.M.C. 1 N.C.O. and 62 Bearers attached to 106 Field Amby for duty	J.W.J.
			7 Other Ranks proceeded on leave. 1 Other Rank R.A.M.C. evacuated sick to C.C.S.	J.W.J.
15/10/18			1 N.C.O. and 2 men at "White Mill" VLAMERTINGHE withdrawn, and this place handed over to I no Corps in accordance with instructions from D.D.M.S. XX Corps	J.W.J.
			12 Other Ranks R.A.M.C. proceeded for duty at Combined Main Dressing Station "ECOLE" YPRES	J.W.J.
16/10/18			Nothing to report	J.W.J.
17/10/18			" " "	J.W.J.
18/10/18			" " "	J.W.J.

WAR DIARY
or
INTELLIGENCE SUMMARY.

(Erase heading not required.)

Army Form C. 2118.

Place	Date	Hour	Summary of Events and Information	Remarks and references to Appendices
BRANDHOEK	28/9/18		105 Field Ambulance took over the Advanced Dressing Station GHELUVELT.	J.W.J.
28/9.10.d-7.7			Shut 28 (J.21.d.1.1) from 106 Field Amb^{ce} and then formed a	
			Main Dressing Station. Opening at 12 noon. Officer :- Major J. W. INNES	J.W.J.
			R.A.M.C. 4.O., Capt S. POTTER R.A.M.C. Lieut J. W. COPELAND M.C. U.S.A.	J.W.J.
			Field Amb^{ce} Bearer Sqds moved to the "ECOLE" YPRES (Shut 28.I.9.c) relieving	J.W.J.
			140 th Field Amb^{ce} at 12.0 noon.	
			4 Other Ranks admitted on leave.	J.W.J.
			5 Other Ranks proceeded on leave.	J.W.J.
ECOLE YPRES	28/9/18		Major J.W.INNES relieved J.W. COPELAND and 15 Other Ranks proceeded from the	J.W.J.
28/I.9.c	9/9/18		Main Dressing Stn 28/J.21.d.1.11 and opened a Main Dressing Stn at BISSEGHEM.	J.W.J.
			Shut 29/J. 9.35.a.8.2	J.W.J.
			4 Other Ranks proceeded on leave.	J.W.J.
	29/9/18		Field Ambulance moved from the "ECOLE" YPRES to BISSEGHEM	J.W.J.
			arriving at 12.00 hrs	
			4 Other Ranks admitted on leave	J.W.J.
			54771 Cpl. ANDERSON. J. M.M. R.A.M.C. awarded Bar to Military Medal	
			for gallantry and devotion to duty in action	
			Lieut. F. WALTON R.A.M.C. rejoined this Unit from 157 Bde R.F.A.	J.W.J.
BISSEGHEM	29/9/18		Capt S. POTTER R.A.M.C. assumed the charge of personnel at GHELUVELT	J.W.J.
29/J.9.35.a.8.2			joined Ad. Amb^{ce} stage at BISSEGHEM	
	2/10/18		13 Other Ranks admitted on leave.	J.W.J.

WAR DIARY
or
INTELLIGENCE SUMMARY.

Army Form C. 2118.

Place	Date	Hour	Summary of Events and Information	Remarks and references to Appendices
BISSEGHEM 29/9.35.8.2.	21/9/18		1 Othr. Rank RAMC posted to this Unit for duty	J.W.9.
			2 N.C.O. and 3 men proceeded for duty on the Light Railway Ambe Trains evacuating from the Main Dist Stn MOORSEELE	J.W.9.
	22/9/18		3 Lorry loads of Stretchers, Blankets etc brought from the ECOLE	J.W.9.
			YPRES and R.A.M.C. Dump formed at BISSEGHEM	J.W.9.
	23/9/18		Lieut J.W. COPELAND, M.C. U.S.A. detailed to visit HEULE daily for the purpose of attending civilian sick	J.W.9.
			Another load of Medical Equipment brought from YPRES to Dump at BISSEGHEM	J.W.9.
	24/9/18		Capt. R.W.B. GIBSON R.A.M.C. rejoined this Unit from 19th Northumberland Fus.	J.W.9.
			14 Othr Ranks proceeded on leave	J.W.9.
			2 " " evacuated sick to C.C.S.	J.W.9.
			Remainder of Equipment brought from YPRES and NINE ELMS to BISSINGHEM	J.W.9.
	25/9/18		1 Othr. Rank evacuated sick	J.W.9.
	26/9/18		Nothing to report	J.W.9.
	27/9/18		1 Othr. Rank evacuated sick	J.W.9.
			13 Othr Ranks proceeded on leave	J.W.9.
	28/9/18		Lieut J.W. COPELAND. M.C. U.S.A. proceeded for duty with 16th Cheshire Regt	J.W.9.
	29/9/18		1 Othr. Rank A.S.C. H.T. posted to this Unit	J.W.9.
	30/9/18		106 Field Amb's moved to SWEVEGHEM taking over the School	J.W.9.
			erected by 106 Field Amb's and opening up as the Main Dressing Station at 16.00 Hrs (See of Instr of Shut 29 (0.1.d 2.6)	J.W.9.

WAR DIARY
or
INTELLIGENCE SUMMARY.

(Erase heading not required.)

Army Form C. 2118.

Place	Date	Hour	Summary of Events and Information	Remarks and references to Appendices
SWEVEGHEM 29 (O.I.d.2.b)	30/10/18		Lieut E. WALTON. R.A.M.C. (S.R.) evacuated sick to 3rd Australian C.C.S.	J.W.J.
		13 o'clock	Other Ranks proceeded on leave.	J.W.J.
	31/10/18		Capt. R.W.B. GIBSON R.A.M.C. (T.C.) proceeded for duty with 15th Regiment. J.W.J.	
			relieving Lieut J.W. COPELAND M.O.R.C. U.S.A. who returned to this Unit.	
			Personnel employed on Light Railway Amb-Trams MOORSEELE returned to this Unit.	J.W.J.
			47098 Sgt KEYWORTH G R.A.M.C. posted to this Unit.	J.W.J.
			Capt S. POTTER R.A.M.C. detailed to run sick daily at transport lines	J.W.J.
			17th Royal Scots and 18th Highland Light Inf.	
			On this attack being launched by 35th Divn our 105 Field Amb was	
			responsible for the Main Dressing Station. The number of	
			cases passed through up to 18.00 hrs were as follows:-	
			13 Officers 210 Other Ranks Germans 1 Officer 19 Other Ranks	J.W.J.

J.W. Inness
Major R.A.M.C.
for O.O. 105TH FIELD AMBULANCE.

CONFIDENTIAL.

W.A R D I A R Y

OF

105th. FIELD AMBULANCE

R.A.M.C.

1st. NOVEMBER 1918

TO

30th. NOVEMBER 1918.

INCLUSIVE.

VOLUME XXXIV.   ORIGINAL.

Army Form C. 2118.

WAR DIARY
or
INTELLIGENCE SUMMARY.
(Erase heading not required.)

Instructions regarding War Diaries and Intelligence Summaries are contained in F. S. Regs., Part II. and the Staff Manual respectively. Title pages will be prepared in manuscript.

Place	Date	Hour	Summary of Events and Information	Remarks and references to Appendices
SWEVEGHEM	4/11/18		Lieut J. W. COPELAND. M.C.U.S.A. proceeded for duty with the 3rd Bn Irish	C/18
Shed 29			Rgt and struck off the strength	
C.1.d.9.10			1. Other Rank admitted wounded	C/18
	5/11/18		1 Other Ranks wounded on duty	C/18
	5/11/18		Nothing to report	C/18
	6/11/18		"	C/18
			8 Other Ranks proceeded on leave	
			Amb. Hd. Qrs. (attached to 106 Fd Amb.) at Advanced Dressing Station	24/7.7.42.7
"	7/11/18		Capt. E. POTTER. R.A.M.C. (T.S.) proceeded for temporary duty with	C/17
			C.R.E. 35 W British Div.	
			One Bearer Squad attached to "B" Coy 19th Durham Light Inf. proceeded	
"	8/11/18		106 Field Amb. H'ters moved to STACEGHEM on H. 30. c.5.6.9. arriving at	C/18
			noon and opening a Main Dressing Station	
STACEGHEM	"		Lieut E. W. STONE. N.C.U.S.A. proceeded for duty as R.M.O. to 10th Bn Durham	C/18
on H.30.c.5.6.9.	8/11/18		Light Inf. relieving Capt. J.T. HILL. R.A.M.C. (T.S.) who returned to this Unit	
	9/11/18		40 Other Ranks wounded on duty	C/18
			The following men awarded the Military Medal for gallantry and	
			devotion to duty in action	
			63713 Pte Singleton B. R.A.M.C. 63692 Pte LINGARD A. R.A.M.C.	
			63692 Pte	

WAR DIARY or INTELLIGENCE SUMMARY

Army Form C. 2118.

Place	Date	Hour	Summary of Events and Information	Remarks and references to Appendices
STACEGHEM	9/4/18		Capt R.W.B. GIBSON. R.A.M.C. (T.C.) proceeded for duty as R.M.O. to 1st Bn. 23rd Public EWB	EWB
29/H.30.c.5.9.			Regt 30/10/18 and is struck off the strength.	
			Lieut F.W. SLOANE. M.C. U.S.A. who proceeded on nyse. for duty with 12th Highland Light Inf. is struck off the strength.	
"	10/4/18		Major D.T. VALENTINE. M.C. R.A.M.C. Ward + 2 Other Ranks attached to 106 Field Ambulance for duty.	EWB
"	"		105 Field Ambulance provided to INGOYGHEM. Abut 21 (23.A.4.7)	
			arriving at 15.00 hrs and staying as a Main Dressing Station.	
INGOYGHEM	11/4/18		13 Other Ranks proceeded on leave.	EWB
29/F.5.A.9.	29/4/18		Lieut F.W. STONE M.C. U.S.A. afforded to this unit from 12th Highland Light Inf. and taken on the strength.	EWB
			3 Other Ranks evacuated sick and struck off strength.	
"	12/4/18		105 Field Ambulance moved to BERCHEM Abut 29 (2.Q.b.9.27) arriving at 14.00 hrs.	EWB
			1 Officer and 2 Other Ranks allowed for 106 Field Amb.	
			11 Other Ranks proceeded on leave.	
BERCHEM	14/4/18		Major D.T. VALENTINE M.C. R.A.M.C. proceeded on leave.	EWB
29/Q.21.d.9.27			Capt J.T. HILL. R.A.M.C. (T.C.) proceeded for duty as M.O. to 11th Lancs. Fus.	EWB
	10/4/18		1/H.Q.M. Sgn. Sgt. Major E.L. PENN. (A.S.C. H.T.) transferred from M.C. & Bns. of.	
			30th Div'l Train and taken on the strength.	

WAR DIARY
or
INTELLIGENCE SUMMARY.

Army Form C. 2118.

Place	Date	Hour	Summary of Events and Information	Remarks and references to Appendices
BERCHEM	17/11/18		3 Other Ranks evacuated sick and struck off the strength	EuB
	20/9 & 21		The following men awarded the Military Medal for gallantry and devotion to duty in action.	
			84947 Pte FRANCIS A.W. R.A.M.C. 29586 Pte POINTER A.B. R.A.M.C.	
	18/11/18		Nothing to report	EuB
	19/11/18		105 Field Amb. moved to HEULE arriving at 19.00 hrs	EuB
			Sick collected from 105 Inf Bde.	
HEULE	20/11/18		1 Other Rank wounded not severe.	EuB
			Lieut E.B. PEACE M.C. U.S.A posted to this Unit and taken on the strength	EuB
			1 Other Rank	
	21/11/18		Nothing to report.	EuB
	22/11/18		Capt T. HILL R.A.M.C. (T.C.) transferred as R.M.O. 17th Lancs Fus	EuB
			on 10/11/18 and struck off the strength.	
	23/11/18		Capt B. POTTER R.A.M.C. returned to this Unit from C.R.E. 35th Div.	EuB
	23/11/18		Lieut E.B. PEACE M.C. U.S.A. proceeded for temporary duty as M.O. of 32 Labour Group.	EuB
	23/11/18		Nothing to report.	EuB
	24/11/18		" " "	EuB
	25/11/18		" " "	EuB
	26/11/18		Move to ST. OMER - WATTEN Area commenced. 105 Field Ambulance	EuB
			moving under orders issued by 105 Infantry Brigade arrived	
			at MENIN at 13.00 hrs	
			Sick collected from 105 Inf Bde.	

Army Form C. 2118.

WAR DIARY
or
INTELLIGENCE SUMMARY.
(Erase heading not required.)

Place	Date	Hour	Summary of Events and Information	Remarks and references to Appendices
MENIN	29/4/18		105 Field Ambulance moving with 105th Inf. Bde arrived at VLAMERTINGHE at 15.30 Hrs. Sick collected from 105 Inf Bde.	O.i.B
VLAMERTINGHE	30/4/18		105 Field Amb. moving with 105th Inf Bdy arrived at STEENVOORDE at 16.00 Hrs. Sick collected from 105 Inf Bde.	O.i.B.

E.W.Stone Lt. M.C.U.S.A.
For O.C. 105 Fd Amb.

CONFIDENTIAL.

---- W A R D I A R Y. ----

OF

---- 105th F I E L D A M B U L A N C E. ----
R. A. M. C.

FROM

---- 1st DECEMBER 1918. ----

TO

---- 31st DECEMBER 1918. ----

INCLUSIVE

VOLUME. XXXV.   ORIGINAL.

WAR DIARY
or
INTELLIGENCE SUMMARY.
(Erase heading not required.)

Army Form C. 2118.

Instructions regarding War Diaries and Intelligence Summaries are contained in F. S. Regs., Part II. and the Staff Manual respectively. Title pages will be prepared in manuscript.

Place	Date	Hour	Summary of Events and Information	Remarks and references to Appendices
STEENVOORDE	1/9/18		105 Field Ambulance continued to move with 105 Infantry Brigade proceeded to PELDERHOUCK (arriving) at 18.00 hours.	S.V.
PELDERHOUCK	2/9/18		105 Field Ambulance proceeded to WATTEN (Chef. ent. 89 ONER Combined Shut 40.000 (L.R. of g.a.) arriving at 4.00 hours.	S.V.
WATTEN (L.W.a.9.9)	3/9/18		Arrangements made for collecting sick daily from 105 Inf Brigade.	S.V.
"	4/9/18		1 O.R. (R.A.M.C.) posted to this Unit. 1 O.R. (R.A.M.C.) evacuated sick.	S.V.
"	5/9/18		Capt. R.W.B. GIBSON. R.A.M.C. (T.C.) rejoined this Unit and taken on strength. 1 O.R. (R.A.M.C.) posted to this Unit.	S.V.
"	6/9/18		Arrangements made for lectures to be given daily on Educational Subjects. Capt. R.W.B. GIBSON. R.A.M.C. granted leave to United Kingdom from 6/9/18 to Lt. E.W. STONE. M.C. U.S. proceeded for temporary duty as M.O. I/c 35th Div Reception Camp.	S.V.
"	7/9/18		Baron de Turen a L'ordre Regiment awarded to 55272 Pte GRAY W. R.A.M.C. 1 O.R. proceeded on leave.	S.V.
"	8/9/18		Lieut. E.W. STONE, M.C. U.S. rejoined this Unit from 35th Div Reception Camp 1 O.R. A.S.C. (H.T.) posted to this Unit.	S.V.
"	9/9/18		Capt. S. POTTER. R.A.M.C. (T.C.) proceeded for temporary duty as M.O. I/c 86th Brigade R.G.A.	S.V.
"	10/9/18		Nothing to report	S.V.
"	11/9/18		"	S.V.
"	12/9/18		"	S.V.

WAR DIARY
or
INTELLIGENCE SUMMARY.
(Erase heading not required.)

Army Form C. 2118.

Place	Date	Hour	Summary of Events and Information	Remarks and references to Appendices
WATTEN (LIH.a.9.9)	12/9/19		3 O.R.s (R.A.M.C.) proceeded for demobilization as coalminers and struck off the strength.	A.V.
	14/9/19		3 O.R.s (R.A.M.C.) proceeded for demobilization as pitmen on stuck off strength	A.V.
	15/9/19		1 O.R. (R.A.M.C.) proceeded for demobilization and struck off the strength.	A.V.
			1 O.R. (R.A.M.C.) evacuated sick.	A.V.
	16/9/19		1 O.R. proceeded on leave	A.V.
	17/9/19		No. 51885 Cpl Nathaniel J. R.A.M.C. proceeded for duty at XIX Corps Staging Camp HAZEBROUCK	A.V.
	18/9/19		Lieut. E.W. STONE M.C.U.S evacuated sick to No. 3 Canadian General Hospital	A.V.
	9/9/19		35 L Division Comfort Composition for 35th Batt'n M.G.C. and Field Amb'ce in which this Unit came second with 897 marks out of 1100.	A.V.
			Lieut. F. WALTON. R.A.M.C. (S.R.) evacuated sick to United Kingdom	
	20/9/19		2 O.R.s/18 and struck off strength. The collection of sick from 105 Inf. Bde. discontinued. From this date 105 B'de Ambulance collects sick daily from 104 and 106 Inf Bdes, 35th Divn. Sub'n 203 & 205 Field Coy R.E. No. 1 2 and 3 Coys. 35th Dvn Train and 2 Coys 35th Batt'n Machine Gun Coy.	A.V. A.V.
	21/9/19		1 O.R. A&S. H.T. evacuated sick.	A.V.
	22/9/19		Lieut. B. Spike R.A.M.C. Nursing proceeded on leave to the United Kingdom this day. Major D. F. Valentine R.A.M.C. (S.R.) assumes temporary	A.V.

WAR DIARY
or
INTELLIGENCE SUMMARY.
(Erase heading not required.)

Army Form C. 2118.

Instructions regarding War Diaries and Intelligence Summaries are contained in F. S. Regs., Part II. and the Staff Manual respectively. Title pages will be prepared in manuscript.

Place	Date	Hour	Summary of Events and Information	Remarks and references to Appendices
WATTEN (L.H.a.99.)	22/9/18		2 O.R.s granted leave to United Kingdom. 1 O.R. (A.S.C. H.T.) posted to this Unit and taken on the strength.	A.V.
	23/9/18		1 officer and 2 men proceeded to take over R.A.M.C. Dump at PELDERHOEK	A.V.
	23/9/18		1 O.R. A.S.C. H.T. posted to this Unit	A.V.
	24/9/18		Nothing to report	
	25/9/18		Pte. J. F. BRIDGE. R.A.M.C. (V.C.) posted to this Unit and taken on strength	A.V.
	25/9/18		1 O.R. R.A.M.C. evacuated sick and struck off the strength.	A.V.
	25/9/18		4 O.R.s (R.A.M.C.) and 1 O.R. (A.S.C. H.T.) proceeded for demobilization and struck off strength	A.V.
	25/9/18		1 O.R. A.S.C. H.T. posted to this Unit and taken on strength.	
	26/9/18		30610 Pte. DONNELLY. F. R.A.M.C. awarded 90 days F.P. No 2. by F.G.C.M. for drunkenness	
			63296 Pte. THORPE. J. R.A.M.C. awarded 60 days F.P. No 2 by F.G.C.M. for drunkenness	
			63814 Pte. GIBBONS. J. R.A.M.C. proceeded to A.M.F.O. WIZERNES, for temp duty	A.V.
			1/4994 Acting Lance Corporal F. L. PENN. A.S.C. H.T. transferred to 1st Dust. Supply and struck off the strength.	A.V.
	28/9/18		Nothing to report	
	29/9/18		Lt. E/B PEACE, M.C. U.S transferred as M.O. to 32 Labour Group officers and struck off strength	A.V.
			1 O.R. (A.S.C. H.T.) proceeded on leave	

Army Form C. 2118.

WAR DIARY
or
INTELLIGENCE SUMMARY.
(Erase heading not required.)

Instructions regarding War Diaries and Intelligence Summaries are contained in F. S. Regs., Part II. and the Staff Manual respectively. Title pages will be prepared in manuscript.

Place	Date	Hour	Summary of Events and Information	Remarks and references to Appendices
WATTEN (L14 a 9.9.)	30/9/18		1.D.R. R.A.M.C. posted to this Unit and taken on the strength. Capt. S. POTTER R.A.M.C. (T.C.) rejoined this Unit from 18 C.C.S. Brigade R.G.A.	D.V.
	3/10/18		Major J.W. INNES R.A.M.C. (T.C.) being unfit to return to France at the resumption of his leave, is Struck off the strength from 10/10/18 inclusive (Auth: D.G.M.S. War Office 24/4/14 (A.M.D. 1) dated 10/10/18)	D.V.

D.J. Valentine.
Major R.A.M.C.
O.C. 105th FIELD AMBULANCE.

CONFIDENTIAL.

35 DIV
Box 2272

WAR DIARY

OF

105TH. FIELD AMBULANCE. R. A. M. C.

FROM

1ST. JANUARY 1919.

TO

31ST. JANUARY 1919.

INCLUSIVE.

VOLUME. XXXVI   ORIGINAL.

WAR DIARY
or
INTELLIGENCE SUMMARY.
(Erase heading not required.)

Army Form C. 2118.

Place	Date	Hour	Summary of Events and Information	Remarks and references to Appendices
WATTEN.	1/1/19		Capt. J.F. BRIDGE. R.A.M.C. proceeded as M.O. 15th Cheshires and 15th Sherwood Foresters. Lieut. E.H. STONE. M.C. U.S.A. evacuated sick to 'UK', and struck off strength as from 18/12/1918.	
	2/1/19		Six Other Ranks R.A.M.C. proceeded to 'UK' for demobilization, and struck off strength. Capt. 2/M. C.F. TYSON. R.A.M.C. mentioned in Sir Douglas Haig's despatches of 8/11/1918.	
	3/1/19		Capt. J.F. BRIDGE. R.A.M.C. struck off strength of this Unit. One Other Rank. R.A.M.C. proceeded for demobilization, and struck off strength.	
	4/1/19		Two Other Ranks. R.A.M.C. proceeded for demobilization, and struck off strength. One Other Rank. R.A.M.C. evacuated sick, and struck off strength.	
	5/1/19		Nothing to report.	
	6/1/19		Temp. Lieut. & 2/M. C.F. TYSON. R.A.M.C. to be Temp. Capt. & 2/Master., vide - London Gazette dated 2/1/1919. One Other Rank R.A.M.C. granted special leave to UK from 6/1/19 to 20/1/19. 1m.068. A/Lt/gl. Major J. Shepard., R.A.S.C. H.T. posted to this Unit for duty, and taken on strength.	C.S.
	7/1/19		Nothing to report.	

Army Form C. 2118.

WAR DIARY
or
INTELLIGENCE SUMMARY.
(Erase heading not required.)

Instructions regarding War Diaries and Intelligence Summaries are contained in F. S. Regs., Part II. and the Staff Manual respectively. Title pages will be prepared in manuscript.

Place	Date	Hour	Summary of Events and Information	Remarks and references to Appendices
HATTEN.	8/1/19		1. N.C.O. R.A.M.C. granted special leave to UK from 8/1/19 to 22/1/19.	
	9/1/19		Nothing to report.	
	10/1/19		Nothing to report.	
	11/1/19		Capt. & Master C.F.TYSON. R.A.M.C. awarded Belgian Croix de Guerre.	
	12/1/19		Inspection of all animals by Remount Board for classification.	
	13/1/19		Nothing to report.	
	14/1/19		Nothing to report.	
	15/1/19		1. Other Rank. proceeded to A.D.M.S. 35th Division for duty as Clerk	
	16/1/19		Capt. & Master C.F.TYSON R.A.M.C. proceeded to UK for demobilization.	
	17/1/19		Seven Other Ranks proceeded for demobilization.	
	18/1/19		Nothing to report.	
	19/1/19		Twenty five Other Ranks, R.A.M.C. proceeded for temporary duty with No.K. Stationary Hospital.	
	20/1/19		Nothing to report.	
	21/1/19		T.40068 S/Sgt./Major J. Shepard. R.A.S.C.H.T. granted leave to UK from 21/1/19 to 4/2/19.	
	22/1/19		Lieut Col. C.SCAIFE. R.A.M.C. returned from leave, and resumes command of the Unit.	C.S.

Army Form C. 2118.

WAR DIARY
or
INTELLIGENCE SUMMARY.
(Erase heading not required.)

Instructions regarding War Diaries and Intelligence Summaries are contained in F. S. Regs., Part II. and the Staff Manual respectively. Title pages will be prepared in manuscript.

Place	Date	Hour	Summary of Events and Information	Remarks and references to Appendices
HATTEN	23/1/19		No. 90454 2.M.2.Q. Abay R.A.M.C. and No. M2031 bn't Sgt. Q.E. Wilson R.A.S.C. M.T. awarded the Meritorious Service Medal. Vide London Gazette dd. 18/1/19.	
	24/1/19		Nothing to report.	
	25/1/19		Major D.I. VALENTINE. M.C. R.A.M.C. granted special leave to U.K. from 25/1/19 to 7/2/19.	
	26/1/19		Nothing to report.	
	27/1/19		One Other Rank R.A.S.C. M.T. transferred to No. 16 G.H.Q. Reserve M.T. Coy 18/1/19, and struck off strength as from that date.	
	28/1/19		Capt R.H.B. GIBSON. R.A.M.C. proceeded to 107d Field Ambulance for temporary duty.	
	29/1/19		Lieut. Col. C. SCAIFE. R.A.M.C. and 70 Other Ranks proceeded to CALAIS for temporary duty.	
	30/1/19		1 N.C.O. 1 man proceeded to U.K. via BOULOGNE, 15/1/19, for demobilization, and struck off strength as from that date.	
	31/1/19		Nothing to report.	

Scott
Lieut. Col. R.A.M.C.
O.O. 105TH FIELD AMBULANCE.

CONFIDENTIAL.

WAR DIARY

OF

105th. FIELD AMBULANCE. RAMC

FROM

1st. FEBRUARY 1919.

TO

28th. FEBRUARY 1919.

INCLUSIVE.

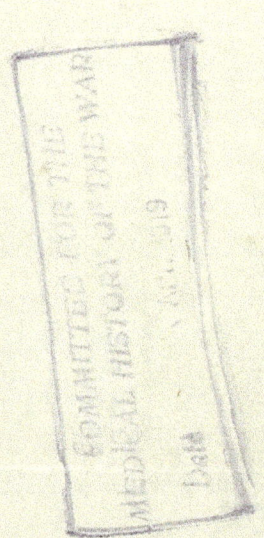

VOLUME XXXVII.   ORIGINAL

Army Form C. 2118.

WAR DIARY
or
INTELLIGENCE SUMMARY.
(Erase heading not required.)

Instructions regarding War Diaries and Intelligence Summaries are contained in F. S. Regs. Part II. and the Staff Manual respectively. Title pages will be prepared in manuscript.

Place	Date	Hour	Summary of Events and Information	Remarks and references to Appendices
WATTEN	1/2/19		Nothing to report.	
	2/2/19		One Other Rank R.A.M.C. demobilized 20/1/19, whilst on leave to U.K. and struck off strength, as from that date. Five Other Ranks R.A.M.C. embarked at Havre 23/1/19 for demobilization, and struck off strength. Capt. R.H.B. GIBSON R.A.M.C. rejoined from 107th Field Ambulance. Lt.Col. C. SCAIFE R.A.M.C. and 10 Other Ranks rejoin from temporary duty at CALAIS.	
	3/2/19		Nothing to report.	
	4/2/19		Four Drivers R.A.S.C.H.T. reported to 35th Divisional Train, as surplus to the new establishment of a Field Ambulance.	
	5/2/19		Capt. S. POTTER R.A.M.C. proceeds for temporary duty as R.M.O. 12th & 18th Battns. Highland Light Infantry.	
	6/2/19		One Other Rank R.A.M.C. embarked at Havre 24/1/19 for demobilization, and struck off strength. The following promotions have been approved and take effect from the dates against their names. Authority:- Officer i/c R.A.M.C. Records. No.59/1000/455 dated 21/1/19. Rte. a/Lgt. CART H. R.A.M.C. to be Sergeant from 13/11/19.16. No. 63865. Rte. a/Lgt. GUERINS. A.J. M.M., R.A.M.C. to be Sergeant from 10/9/1916.	

Neate
Lt.Col.

Army Form C. 2118.

WAR DIARY
or
INTELLIGENCE SUMMARY
(Erase heading not required.)

Instructions regarding War Diaries and Intelligence Summaries are contained in F. S. Regs., Part II. and the Staff Manual respectively. Title pages will be prepared in manuscript.

Place	Date	Hour	Summary of Events and Information	Remarks and references to Appendices
WATTEN	6/2/19		No. 18183. Cpl. a/L.Cpl COOPER. C.B. R.A.M.C. to be Temp/y Sergeant from 31/1/1916.	
			No. 63804. Pte a/Lpl WHISKER. T.G. R.A.M.C. to be Sergeant from 12/4/1916.	
			No. 63873. Pte. a/Cpl TAAFFE T. M.M., R.A.M.C. to be Corporal from 12/2/1918.	
	7/2/19		One Other Rank R.A.M.C. granted special leave to U.K. from 5/2/19 to 19/2/19.	
			Capt. S. POTTER. R.A.M.C. rejoins Unit from 12th + 13th Battn., Highland L.Infy.	
			Capt. + Q.Mr. C.E. TYSON. R.A.M.C. embarked for demobilization 1/4/19, and struck off strength.	
			One Other Rank R.A.M.C. embarked at Boulogne 31/1/19, for demobilisation, and struck off strength.	
			Twelve Other Ranks R.A.M.C. proceed for temporary duty at No. 4. Stationary Hospital.	
			Four Other Ranks R.A.M.C. and One Other Rank R.A.S.C.H.T. proceed for demobilisation.	
	8/2/19		Nothing to report.	
	9/2/19		Capt. R.H.P. GIBSON. R.A.M.C. proceeded for temporary duty as R.M.O. 363 Battn. M.G.C.	
			One Other Rank R.A.S.C.H.T. admitted to Hospital whilst on leave to U.K. on 23/10/1918. and struck off strength.	
	10/2/19		Four Other Ranks R.A.M.C. proceed for demobilisation.	
	11/2/19		Nothing to report.	

V. Agathe
Lieut.

(A7091). Wt. W12859/M1293 75,000. 4/17. D. D. & L. Ltd. Forms/C.2118/14

Army Form C. 2118.

WAR DIARY
or
INTELLIGENCE SUMMARY.
(Erase heading not required.)

Instructions regarding War Diaries and Intelligence Summaries are contained in F. S. Regs., Part II and the Staff Manual respectively. Title pages will be prepared in manuscript.

Place	Date	Hour	Summary of Events and Information	Remarks and references to Appendices
WATTEN	12/2/19		Capt S. POTTER R.A.M.C. proceeds for temporary duty with 106th Field Ambulance. Capt. R.H.B. GIBSON R.A.M.C. rejoins Unit from 35th Battn. M.G.C. One Other Rank R.A.S.C.H.T reposted to 35th Div. Train for duty, as surplus to new establishment of a Field Ambulance. One Other Rank R.A.S.C.N.T. reposted to 35th Div. M.T. Coy	
	13/2/19		Two Other Ranks R.A.M.C. proceed for demobilization. One Other Rank R.A.M.C. granted leave to U.K. from 13/2/19 to 27/2/19. One Other Rank R.A.M.C. evacuated sick to Base 8/2/19 a struck off strength	
	14/2/19		Capt R.H.B.GIBSON R.A.M.C. evacuated sick to No4 Staty Hospital. One Other Rank R.A.M.C. evacuated sick to No 4 Staty. Hospital 12/2/19 and struck off strength.	
	15/2/19		Nothing to report.	
	16/2/19		Four Other Ranks R.A.M.C. proceed for demobilization.	
	17/2/19		Nothing to report.	
	18/2/19		Nothing to report.	
	19/2/19		Fifteen Other Ranks R.A.M.C. proceed to 106th Field Ambulance for temporary duty. Three Other Ranks R.A.M.C. proceed for demobilization.	
	23/2/19		One "P.B." man attached R.P.S.C.H.T. proceeds for demobilization.	

Army Form C. 2118.

WAR DIARY
or
INTELLIGENCE SUMMARY.
(Erase heading not required.)

Instructions regarding War Diaries and Intelligence Summaries are contained in F. S. Regs., Part II. and the Staff Manual respectively. Title pages will be prepared in manuscript.

Place	Date	Hour	Summary of Events and Information	Remarks and references to Appendices
WATTEN.	20/2/19		One Other Rank R.A.M.C. granted special leave to U.K. from 20/2/19 to 6/3/19.	
	21/2/19		Nothing to report.	
	22/2/19		One Other Rank R.A.M.C. re-posted to this Unit, on discharge from Hospital, and retaken on strength. Three Other Ranks R.A.M.C. proceed for demobilization.	
	23/2/19		One Other Rank R.A.M.C. embarked 13/2/19 for demobilization, and struck off strength. One Other Rank R.A.M.C. embarked 14/2/19 for demobilization and struck off strength. Two Other Ranks R.A.M.C. embarked 15/2/19 for demobilization, and struck off strength. Four Other Ranks R.A.S.C.H.T. proceed for demobilization.	
	24/2/19		Nothing to report.	
	25/2/19		One Other Rank R.A.M.C. evacuated sick to No. 4 Staty. Hospital, and struck off strength. Four Other Ranks R.A.M.C. proceed for demobilization.	
	26/2/19		Nothing to report.	
	27/2/19		One Other Rank R.A.M.C. granted special leave to U.K. from 27/2/19 to 13/3/19. Three Other Ranks R.A.M.C. proceed for demobilization.	

WAR DIARY or ~~INTELLIGENCE SUMMARY~~

Army Form C. 2118.

Place	Date	Hour	Summary of Events and Information	Remarks and references to Appendices
WATTEN.	27/2/19		Lieut Col. C. SCAIFE. R.A.M.C. assumes temporary duty as A.D.M.S. 35th Division during absence of Col. H.L. STEELE. A.M.S. on leave to U.K.	
	28/2/19		Capt. R.N.B.GIBSON. R.A.M.C. evacuated sick to ENGLAND 25/2/19. and struck off strength.	

Scaife
Lieut Col. R.A.M.C.
O.C. 106th Field Ambulance.

CONFIDENTIAL.

WAR DIARY

OF

105th. FIELD AMBULANCE

FROM

1st. MARCH 1919.

TO

31st. MARCH 1919,

INCLUSIVE.

VOLUME. XXXVIII.   ORIGINAL.

Army Form C. 2118.

WAR DIARY
or
INTELLIGENCE SUMMARY.
(Erase heading not required.)

Instructions regarding War Diaries and Intelligence Summaries are contained in F.S. Regs., Part II. and the Staff Manual respectively. Title pages will be prepared in manuscript.

Place	Date	Hour	Summary of Events and Information	Remarks and references to Appendices
WATTEN.	1/3/19		3 Other Ranks R.A.M.C. embarked at BOULOGNE 12/2/19, and struck off strength.	
			3 Other Ranks R.A.M.C. embarked at BOULOGNE 17/2/19, and struck off strength.	
			CAPT. H.R.M. TURTLE. R.A.M.C. posted to this Unit and taken on strength.	
	2/3/19		4 "P.B" men attached R.A.S.C.H.T. proceed for demobilization.	
			1 Other Rank R.A.M.C. proceed for duty at Office of D.D.M.S. XIX Corps.	
			22 "J" class animals proceed to Fifth Army Animal Collecting Camp ARQUES.	
	3/3/19		No. 32048. Sgt Major A.H. APPLEBY., R.A.M.C. and two Other Ranks R.A.M.C. proceed for demobilization.	
	4/3/19		Nothing to report.	
	5/3/19		CAPT. H.R.M. TURTLE. R.A.M.C. transferred to 106th Field Ambulance, and struck off strength.	
			1 Other Rank R.A.M.C. embarked at BOULOGNE 20/3/19 for demobilization, and struck off strength.	
			2 Other Ranks R.A.M.C. embarked at BOULOGNE 24/2/19, for demobilization, and struck off strength.	
			1 Other Rank R.A.M.C. embarked at BOULOGNE 25/2/19, for demobilization, and struck off strength.	

Army Form C. 2118.

WAR DIARY
or
INTELLIGENCE SUMMARY.
(Erase heading not required.)

Instructions regarding War Diaries and Intelligence Summaries are contained in F. S. Regs., Part II. and the Staff Manual respectively. Title pages will be prepared in manuscript.

Place	Date	Hour	Summary of Events and Information	Remarks and references to Appendices
WATTEN	6/3/19		LIEUT. J.H. COPELAND. M.C. U.S. posted to the Unit for duty, and taken on strength.	
			4 Other Ranks R.A.M.C. proceed for demobilization.	
			1. Other Rank. R.A.M.C. rejoins Unit from D.D.M.S. XIX Corps.	
	7/3/19		Nothing to report.	
	8/3/19		1. Other Rank R.A.M.C. transferred to No 54 b.b.S. and struck off strength.	
			2 Other Ranks R.A.M.C. transferred to A.D.M.S. 3rd Division for duty, and struck off strength.	
			3 Other Ranks R.A.M.C. and 1 Other Rank R.A.S.C.H.T. proceed for demobilization	
	9/3/19		CAPT. S. POTTER. R.A.M.C. posted to 106th Field Ambulance, and struck off strength.	
	10/3/19		Nothing to report.	
	11/3/19		1. Other Rank. R.A.S.C.M.T. demobilized 16/1/19, whilst on leave to U.K., and struck off strength.	
	12/3/19		19. Other Ranks, R.A.M.C. proceed for demobilization.	
			4 "X" class animals despatched to Fifth Army Animal Collecting Camp ARQUES.	
	13/3/19		2 Other Ranks. R.A.M.C. embark at BOULOGNE 21/2/19 for demobilization, and struck off strength.	
			1 Other Rank R.A.M.C. embarked at BOULOGNE 22/2/19 for demobilization, and struck	

Army Form C. 2118.

WAR DIARY
or
INTELLIGENCE SUMMARY.
(Erase heading not required.)

Instructions regarding War Diaries and Intelligence Summaries are contained in F. S. Regs. Part II. and the Staff Manual respectively. Title pages will be prepared in manuscript.

Place	Date	Hour	Summary of Events and Information	Remarks and references to Appendices
WATTEN.	13/3/19		1 Other Rank R.A.M.C. embarked at BOULOGNE 25/2/19 for demobilization, and struck off strength.	
			1 Other Rank R.A.M.C. embarked at BOULOGNE 26/2/19 for demobilization, and struck off strength.	
			2 Other Ranks R.A.M.C. embark at BOULOGNE 27/2/19 for demobilization, and struck off strength.	
			2 Other Ranks R.A.M.C. embark at BOULOGNE 1/3/19 for demobilization, and struck off strength.	
			4 Other Ranks R.A.M.C. embark at BOULOGNE 4/3/19 for demobilization, and struck off strength.	
	14/3/19		1 Other Rank R.A.M.C. evacuated sick to No 4. Stationary Hospital, and struck off strength.	
			1 Other Rank R.A.S.C.M.T. re-posted to 35th Divisional M.T. Coy.	
	16/3/19		20 Other Ranks R.A.M.C. and 1 Other Rank R.A.S.C.H.T. proceed for demobilization.	
			1 Other Rank R.A.M.C. embarked at BOULOGNE 4/3/19 for demobilization, and struck off strength.	

Army Form C. 2118

WAR DIARY
or
INTELLIGENCE SUMMARY
(Erase heading not required.)

Instructions regarding War Diaries and Intelligence Summaries are contained in F. S. Regs., Part II. and the Staff Manual respectively. Title Pages will be prepared in manuscript.

Place	Date	Hour	Summary of Events and Information	Remarks and references to Appendices
WATTEN	16/3/19		1 Other Rank R.A.M.C. transferred to A.D.M.S. 3rd Division for duty, and struck off strength.	
	17/3/19		2 Other Ranks R.A.S.C.H.T. re-posted to 35th Div. Train, and struck off strength.	
			Nothing to report.	
	18/3/19		2 Other Ranks R.A.M.C. proceed for demobilization.	
			6 "X" class animals proceed to Fifth Army Animal Collecting Camp ARQUES.	
	19/3/19		Nothing to report.	
	20/3/19		No. 32048 Sgt Major A.H. APPLEBY, R.A.M.C. and two Other Ranks R.A.M.C. embarked at BOULOGNE 14/3/19, and struck off strength.	
			4 Other Ranks R.A.M.C. embarked at BOULOGNE 15/3/19 for demobilization, and struck off strength.	
	21/3/19		Nothing to report.	
	22/3/19		Nothing to report.	
	23/3/19		Nothing to report.	
	24/3/19		Lieut. J.H. COPELAND, M.C. U.S. transferred to 106th Field Ambulance 10/3/19, and struck off strength.	

1875 Wt. W5593/826 1,000,000 4/15 J.B.C. & A. A.D.S.S./Forms/C. 2118.

Army Form C. 2118

WAR DIARY
or
INTELLIGENCE SUMMARY
(Erase heading not required.)

Instructions regarding War Diaries and Intelligence Summaries are contained in F. S. Regs., Part II. and the Staff Manual respectively. Title Pages will be prepared in manuscript.

Place	Date	Hour	Summary of Events and Information	Remarks and references to Appendices
WATTEN	25/3/19		Nothing to report	
	26/3/19		Under instructions from DDMS XII Corps, Lieut-Col. C. SCAIFE. R.A.M.C. takes over command of No. 11 Casualty Clearing Station. STEENWERCK. and is struck off the strength of this Unit.	
			Major D. J. VALENTINE, M.C. R.A.M.C. assumes command of this Unit, vice, Lieut Col. C. SCAIFE. R.A.M.C.	
			1. Other Rank. R.A.M.C. evacuated sick to No. 4 Stationary Hospital, and struck off strength.	
			1. Other Rank. R.A.M.C. embarked at BOULOGNE 19/3/19 for demobilization, and struck off strength.	
			3. Other Ranks. R.A.M.C. proceed for demobilization.	
			1. Other Rank. R.A.M.C. embarked at BOULOGNE for demobilization 2/3/19 and struck off strength.	
	27/3/19		1. Other Rank. R.A.M.C. embarked at BOULOGNE for demobilization 19/3/19, and struck off strength.	
			1. Other Rank. R.A.M.C. proceed for demobilization.	
			Unit reduced to Cadre Establishment.	

Army Form C. 2118

WAR DIARY
or
INTELLIGENCE SUMMARY
(Erase heading not required.)

Instructions regarding War Diaries and Intelligence Summaries are contained in F.S. Regs., Part II. and the Staff Manual respectively. Title Pages will be prepared in manuscript.

Place	Date	Hour	Summary of Events and Information	Remarks and references to Appendices
HATTEN	28/3/19		Nothing to report	
	29/3/19		Nothing to report	
	30/3/19		1 Other Rank. R.A.M.C. granted special leave to U.K. from 30/3/19 to 13/4/19.	
	31/3/19		1 Other Rank. R.A.M.C. embarked at BOULOGNE for demobilization 19/3/19, and struck off strength.	
			1 Other Rank. R.A.M.C. embarked at BOULOGNE for demobilization 24/3/19, and struck off strength.	

J. Mawkin
Major. R.A.M.C.
Commanding 105th Field Ambulance.

CONFIDENTIAL.

WAR DIARY

OF

105th. FIELD AMBULANCE.

FROM

APRIL 1st. 1919.

TO

APRIL 24th. 1919.

INCLUSIVE.

VOLUME XXXIV.   ORIGINAL

Army Form C. 2118.

WAR DIARY
or
INTELLIGENCE SUMMARY.
(Erase heading not required.)

Instructions regarding War Diaries and Intelligence Summaries are contained in F. S. Regs., Part II. and the Staff Manual respectively. Title pages will be prepared in manuscript.

Place	Date	Hour	Summary of Events and Information	Remarks and references to Appendices
WATTEN	1/4/19		Nothing to report	Of.
	2/4/19		12 Other Ranks R.A.M.C. embark at BOULOGNE 23/3/19 for demobilization, and struck off strength.	
			00454 Q.M.S. A. HAY R.A.M.C. and 8 Other Ranks R.A.M.C. embark at BOULOGNE 24/3/19 for demobilization, and struck off strength.	
			1 Other Rank R.A.M.C. demobilized 30/12/18, whilst on leave to U.K. and struck off strength.	10G.
			1 Other Rank R.A.M.C. demobilized 30/1/19, whilst on leave to U.K., and struck off strength.	10G.
	3/4/19		Nothing to report	
	4/4/19		6 Drivers R.A.S.C.H.T. reported to Hqrs. 35th Divl. Train, and struck off strength.	
			2 P.B. men attached R.A.S.C.H.T. transferred to 227th Divisional Employment Coy. and struck off strength.	
			8 Other Ranks R.A.M.C. embark at BOULOGNE 23/3/19 for demobilization, and struck off strength.	10G.
			1 Other Rank R.A.M.C. embarked at BOULOGNE 23/3/19 for demobilization, and struck off strength.	

Army Form C. 2118.

WAR DIARY
or
INTELLIGENCE SUMMARY
(Erase heading not required.)

Instructions regarding War Diaries and Intelligence Summaries are contained in F. S. Regs., Part II. and the Staff Manual respectively. Title pages will be prepared in manuscript.

Place	Date	Hour	Summary of Events and Information	Remarks and references to Appendices
HATTEN.	4/4/19		8 Other Ranks R.A.M.C. embarked at BOULOGNE 2/4/3/19 for demobilization, and struck off strength.	
			2 Drivers R.A.S.C. H.T. transferred to this Unit for duty from 35d Divl Train, and taken on strength.	
	5/4/19		4 Drivers R.A.S.C. H.T. transferred to this Unit for duty from 35d Divl Train and taken on strength.	
	6/4/19		Nothing to report.	
	7/4/19		Nothing to report.	
	8/4/19		Capt. a/Major H.A. ROWELL, M.C., R.A.M.C., D.A.D.M.S. 35d Division, proceeded to 'UK' for duty and Capt. a/Major D.J. VALENTINE, M.C., R.A.M.C., a/O.C. 105d Field Ambulance assumes duties of S.M.O. 35d Division.	
	9/4/19		Capt. P.A. GALPIN, R.A.M.C.T. transferred to this Unit for duty from No. 10. Stationary Hospital and taken on strength.	
	10/4/19		4 Other Ranks R.A.M.C. embarked at BOULOGNE 1/4/19 for demobilization, and struck off strength.	
			1 Other Rank R.A.S.C.M.T. granted leave to 'UK' from 1/4/19 to 25/4/19.	

Army Form C. 2118.

WAR DIARY
or
INTELLIGENCE SUMMARY.
(Erase heading not required.)

Instructions regarding War Diaries and Intelligence Summaries are contained in F. S. Regs., Part II. and the Staff Manual respectively. Title pages will be prepared in manuscript.

Place	Date	Hour	Summary of Events and Information	Remarks and references to Appendices
WATTEN	11/4/19		No 63,999. Pte SHORT. P.W. R.A.M.C. appointed acting Lance Corporal with pay from 15/2/1919.	
	12/4/19		Nothing to report.	
	13/4/19		Nothing to report.	
	14/4/19		Capt. P.A. GALPIN. R.A.M.C.T. granted special leave to "U.K." from 14/4/19 to 16/4/19.	
	15/4/19		Nothing to report.	
	16/4/19		Nothing to report.	
	17/4/19		MAJOR. D.J. VALENTINE. M.C. R.A.M.C. transferred to 106th Field Ambulance for duty, and struck off strength. Capt. P.A GALPIN R.A.M.C.T. assumed command of Cadre of this Unit vice MAJOR D J VALENTINE M.C. R.A.M.C. 9. Other Ranks R.A.S.C. M.T. reported to 36th Div. M.T. Coy. and struck off strength.	
	18/4/19		1. N.C.O. & 3. Drivers. R.A.S.C. H.T., & 3. Other Ranks. R.A.M.C. proceed with transport to St OMER station for entrainment.	
WATTEN	18/4/19		Capt P.A GALPIN R.A.M.C & Cadre of Field Ambulance proceeds to ST OMER for	

Army Form C. 2118.

WAR DIARY
or
INTELLIGENCE SUMMARY.
(Erase heading not required.)

Instructions regarding War Diaries and Intelligence Summaries are contained in F. S. Regs., Part II. and the Staff Manual respectively. Title pages will be prepared in manuscript.

Place	Date	Hour	Summary of Events and Information	Remarks and references to Appendices
HATTEN	18/4/19		Entrainment for Dunkirk, arrive at Dunkirk 10.30 p.m.	
DUNKIRK	19/4/19		Personnel of Unit go through obtaining passes & move to No 2 Camp DUNKIRK.	
	20/4/19		Nothing to report.	
	21/4/19		Nothing to report.	
	22/4/19		Transport loaded on "S.S. CLUTHA", personnel embark on S.S. VAICATCH	
	23/4/19		"S.S. CLUTHA" & "S.S. VAICATCH" proceed for SOUTHAMPTON, both ships anchor first outside SOUTHAMPTON, arrive at 8.00 p.m.	
	24/4/19		Personnel dis-embark at SOUTHAMPTON, transport unloaded, personnel & transport proceed to Malaria Concentration Centre RIPON, arriving at 2 a.m. 25/4/19.	

W. Gaqin
Captain R.A.M.C.
O.C. 105th Field Ambulance R.A.M.C.

www.ingramcontent.com/pod-product-compliance
Lightning Source LLC
Chambersburg PA
CBHW080908230426
43664CB00016B/2757